I Am Called

Answering the Call of God with a Life on a Mission

Ryan Brooks

Scripture quotations marked (ESV) are taken from the ESV® Bible (The Holy Bible, English Standard Version®). ESV® Text Edition: 2016. Copyright © 2001 by Crossway, a publishing ministry of Good News Publishers. The ESV® text has been reproduced in cooperation with and by permission of Good News Publishers. Unauthorized reproduction of this publication is prohibited. Used by permission. All rights reserved.

Scripture marked (GW) is taken from God's Word®, © 1995 God's Word to the Nations. Used by permission of God's Word Mission Society.

Scripture quotations marked (MSG) are taken from *The Message*, copyright © 1993, 2002, 2018 by Eugene H. Peterson. Used by permission of NavPress. All rights reserved. Represented by Tyndale House Publishers, Inc.

Scripture quotations marked (NASB) are taken from the New American Standard Bible®, Copyright © 1960, 1962, 1963, 1968, 1971, 1972, 1973, 1975, 1977, 1995 by The Lockman Foundation. Used by permission. www.Lockman.org.

Scripture quotations marked (NIV) are taken from the Holy Bible, New International Version®, NIV® Copyright © 1973, 1978, 1984, 2011 by Biblica, Inc.® Used by permission. All rights reserved worldwide.

Scripture quotations marked (NKJV) are taken from the New King James Version®. Copyright © 1982 by Thomas Nelson, Inc. Used by permission. All rights reserved.

Sermon To Book
www.sermontobook.com

I Am Called / Ryan Brooks
ISBN-13: 978-1-952602-28-3

To my wife, April: Your words, thoughts, support, and encouragement mean more to me than any other's. I pray daily that I am a man who makes God proud, but also you proud. I love you so much.

To my children, Darian, Brandon, Wesley, and London: I pray that these words impact your lives. You are my inspiration and my greatest responsibility. I do not take you for granted, and I love you.

To Vertical Church: Thank you for trusting me and giving me the grace to grow in my leadership. Your prayers and support are felt more than you know, and I count the opportunity to pastor you a great privilege.

Pastor Ryan offers an accessible, readable, and faithful exploration of one of the Bible's most interesting characters, Jonah. He shows that Jonah answered a question we all have to face at some point: "Whose voice will I listen to?" Not everything that comes from heaven has your name on it, but something does. Your destiny is determined by whether you hear and heed [God's] voice. You'll find these pages not only challenging and convicting, but encouraging as well. Read this book and share it with someone else!

J.D. Greear, Pastor, Summit Church, Author of *What Are You Going to Do with Your Life?*

If you're wondering what God wants you to do with the life that he has given you, then you should use this book to guide your discernment process. Pastor Ryan Brooks has handcrafted a prophetically powerful and pastorally practical gift.

Matt Adair, Pastor, Christ Community Church, Athens, GA

Pastor Ryan has a passion for gospel understanding and gospel application, and it's painted through words on the pages of this book. *I Am Called* is full of simple yet powerful principles for understanding what it means to live out the gospel for Jesus no matter where you are in your walk with Christ. Every Christian is called to the same mission, but it's lived out in many different ways, and Pastor Ryan helps us figure out what that looks like for us as individuals.

Bryan Loritts, Teaching Pastor, author of *The Dad Difference*

Figuring out your calling and purpose is something that humanity has wrestled with since creation. From podcasts and blogs to books and conferences, people hunt to find a sense of belonging and purpose, but what do you do once the calling question is answered? Ryan Brooks has provided us with the "now what?" of not just understanding your call, but also answering and fulfilling it with joy, aggression, clarity, and passion. When it comes to calling, it's not a question of *whether* you will answer a call, but rather *which* call you will answer. *I Am Called* provides people with the blueprint to realize their God-given design.

Jerome Gay Jr., Lead Pastor, Vision Church, Author of *The Whitewashing of Christianity: A Hidden Past, A Hurtful Present and a Hopeful Future*

Pastor Ryan loves Jesus. Every page drips with love for our King. This book is filled with practical insights and gems that encourage and equip you to live life on mission with Jesus.

Dr. Derwin L. Gray, Co-founder and Lead Elder-Pastor, Transformation Church, Author of *The Good Life: What Jesus Teaches About Finding True Happiness*

Ryan has a rare gift of connecting with ease to people across cultural and generational lines. He is a masterful preacher who lives his sermons, as pastors are called to do. In this book Ryan is inviting others into the joy of what he's found in his pursuit of God's calling on his own life. Read it and discover the joy of being called up to God's mission.

Spence Shelton, Lead Pastor, Mercy Church

Many people go through life unfulfilled. In *I Am Called*, Ryan unpacks how to discover your calling so you can live a fulfilled, fruitful, and focused life.

Terrance H. Johnson, Senior Pastor, Higher Dimension Church, and author of *The Answer*

I've had the honor of working with Ryan for several years. He has the heart of a pastor and the mind of a scholar. This is a great book, with great lessons for anyone who wants to better understand what following God actually looks like.

Michael Lukaszewski, Founder of Church Fuel

CONTENTS

Taking the Call

If you have a cell phone, you have probably faced the dilemma of choosing whether or not to answer a particular call. When certain people call, you may let it ring as many times as you can while you consider the caller, what you are doing, and whether you really have time to talk to the person at that moment. Maybe you know that if you do answer, the discussion is going to be draining, or you know that the caller (hello, 1-800 number!) is just trying to get something from you.

There are certain calls that you know you *must* answer—calls from your mother and your spouse, for example. If I don't answer the phone when my wife calls me, there will be an immediate follow-up text: "Why aren't you answering?"

Every day, God calls us, too. He beckons us, reaches out to us, extends Himself to us, requests and requires of us, and we must decide how we will answer His call. There are corporate calls that are for everyone in the body of Christ. We are all called to share the gospel and to go out and make disciples. But there are also calls for individuals as well as calls for specific seasons in our lives.

> *When it comes to your life's direction, it's not a question of **whether** you will answer a call, but rather **which** call you will answer.*

Sometimes the call is not easy. Sometimes God asks us to go where we are not comfortable. God calls us to sacrifice, to serve, to pursue justice, to seek the good of others, and even to suffer. Let's be clear that what God often calls us to do will not make us popular, famous, or wealthy, but it will be part of His redemptive work in the world. Sometimes He asks us to love those who are hard to love. Why? Because in doing so, we become more like Him.

Jonah was a prophet in the Old Testament who was given such a call. God asked him to do the unthinkable: to go to his nation's most powerful enemy and preach repentance and forgiveness. Jonah was rocked to the core and challenged with something that we are challenged with. Will we obey God's call no matter what the outcome? Will we obey God even when we don't like what He is asking?

A person's decision whether or not to answer God's call in any particular situation directly affects others. *I Am Called* will consider how Jonah's actions impacted both a group of sailors and an entire nation and how our response to God can also have a far-reaching impact.

There will always be voices pulling us to do one thing or another. When it comes to your life's direction, it's not a question of *whether* you will answer a call, but rather *which* call you will answer. Will you answer a voice that may be contradicting God, or will you answer His call? Your choice may be life-changing. Correction: your choice will be life-changing—and not just for your life.

A Note About the Workbook

Following each main chapter of this book is a workbook section, which includes reflective questions, application-oriented action steps, and pages for recording notes. These sections are intended for use in independent reflection, group study, or discussion with a friend as you dedicate yourself to answering God's call obediently and wholeheartedly. Now prepare yourself to grow as a representative of God in the world and help others to restore their relationship with Him through Jesus Christ!

CHAPTER ONE

Answering the Right Call:
What's Calling You, and How Do You Answer?

The word of the LORD came to Jonah son of Amittai: "Go to the great city of Nineveh and preach against it, because its wickedness has come up before me."

But Jonah ran away from the LORD and headed for Tarshish. He went down to Joppa, where he found a ship bound for that port. After paying the fare, he went aboard and sailed for Tarshish to flee from the LORD.
—Jonah 1:1–3 *(NIV)*

When you hear the name "Jonah," what comes to mind? Maybe a cartoon drawing of a guy in Middle Eastern garb being swallowed by a whale? How about a catchy little kids' tune that gets stuck in your head? The little book of Jonah in the Old Testament is a lot more than a children's story. It has powerful lessons for us about answering God's call on our lives, and it challenges our hearts to walk out our lives in light of the gospel.

Jonah, whose name means "dove," lived in the eighth century BC during the reign of an evil Israelite king named Jeroboam. The book of Jonah is not the first time the Bible speaks of this prophet. In 2 Kings 14:25, the Bible says that King Jeroboam II "restored the border of Israel from the entrance of Hamath as far as the Sea of the Arabah, according to the word of the LORD, the God of Israel, which He spoke through His servant Jonah the son of Amittai, the prophet, who was of Gath-hepher" (NASB). In these verses, we learn that Jonah was a prophet.

In the book of Jonah, God's specific call for His prophet was to go to Nineveh and warn its people against their sin, which had engulfed the entire city (Jonah 1:1–2). Unfortunately for Jonah, he chose to turn against God's call. As Jonah 1:3 recounts, he "ran away from the LORD" (NIV). He traveled to the port of Joppa and from there boarded a ship bound for Tarshish.

Again, your life's direction is not a question of whether you will answer a call, but rather which call you will answer. Will you be obedient to the call of God, or will you listen to another voice and obey it rather than God?

How you respond is paramount and will affect your relationship with God and others. Oftentimes my disappointments in life have been because I did not answer the right call. I have answered the call of comfort and ease—the least challenging and least risky—and all the calls voiced by my fears. I listened to my own inner man and answered the call that I thought was right for me instead of seeking God and asking Him, "God, what do You want me to do? Where are You calling me?"

I have come to learn that, like for Jonah, God will set before me both a direction and a decision. Through His

Word, we find direction, but we still must make the decision to follow.

Four Ways God Calls Us

Before we look more deeply into the book of Jonah, it's important to consider the different ways God calls His children. I've identified four for the purpose of this book: identity, destiny, intimacy, and responsibility.

Identity

God calls those He loves by name. Isaiah 43:1 says, "But now, this is what the LORD says—he who created you, Jacob, he who formed you, Israel: 'Do not fear, for I have redeemed you; I have summoned you by name; you are mine'" (NIV). What does it mean that God calls His children by name?

Over and over in the Bible, God called people by name. In several instances, He even changed someone's name: Abram to Abraham (Genesis 17:5) and Sarai to Sarah (Genesis 17:15), for example. In the ancient world—the context in which the Bible was written—a person's name was his or her identity and reflected to others who he or she was. Those God calls by name are described as His own, belonging solely to Him. They are His.

As followers of Christ, we are called the children of God, His sons and daughters. Scripture illuminates our identity in Christ, saying that we are "children of God" (John 1:12 NIV), branches of "the true vine" and conduits of Christ's life (John 15:1, 5 NIV), and His "friends" (John

15:15 NIV). We have been "justified" and redeemed (Romans 3:24 NIV). We are "no longer ... slaves to sin" because we have been crucified with Christ (Romans 6:6 NIV) and "set ... free from the law of sin and death" (Romans 8:2 NIV). Those who trust Jesus are called "saints" (1 Corinthians 1:2 ESV). We are wise, righteous, and sanctified (1 Corinthians 1:30). The moment we understand who Jesus is and believe, we receive everything that identifies who we are in Christ. This is our new name!

When Jesus identified Simon as Peter, He called him *Petros,* or "rock," indicating that Simon (Peter) would be solid and stand firm. He gave him an identity—not who he used to be, but the man he was going to become. God often changed people's names because He was repurposing them, changing their identity from how the world saw them to how God sees them. Let's never forget that when we give our lives to Jesus Christ, we have a new identity in Him (2 Corinthians 5:17). Salvation gives us a new identity in Christ, and that changes everything.

Destiny

In simple terms, a person's destiny is God's purpose for his or her life. It is His appointed or ordained future, set before the beginning of time. Your destiny is what God has predetermined you to become. In the Old Testament, that destiny might have been to be a king, a priest, a prophet, a worshipper, or a tentmaker.

Romans 8:29 clarifies, "For those God foreknew he also predestined *to be conformed to the image of his Son"* (NIV, emphasis added). In Christ, all of our individual destinies are rolled up into one magnificent purpose: to be like Him. This destiny is not based on any work the individual does, but on his or her identity as a child of God.

Romans 8:28 says, "And we know that God causes all things to work together for good to those who love God, to those who are called according to His purpose" (NASB). Our destiny becomes His purpose for us.

Intimacy

Many assume that the first mention of Jonah in the Bible is in the book of Jonah. The first time I heard the story of Jonah, I figured that he was hanging out at the mall or somewhere, and the Lord said, "Hey, guess what? I've picked you to be a prophet. Here is what I want you to do…." But as we have seen, Jonah is first mentioned in 2 Kings 14:25. He was already a successful prophet of God when God directed him to Nineveh. Jonah already had a relationship with his Creator.

God longs to relate with His people. He longs for His people to know Him, to "grope for Him and find Him" (Acts 17:27 NASB). Revelation 3:20 says, "Behold, I stand at the door and knock. If anyone hears my voice and opens the door, I will come in to him and eat with him, and he with me" (ESV). It's impossible to have a deep friendship with someone without knowing that person personally.

Many people believe that God wants something from them, but what He really wants is relationship. Adam sinned, creating separation between God and man. However, God sent Jesus as the ultimate sacrifice to redeem and reconcile man back to God for relationship and fellowship. That is His utmost priority for each of us.

Responsibility

Our actions and work matter, but they only come after intimacy. A byproduct of a relationship with God will be ways you can help with His purpose of redemption and reconciliation. When you walk with God, your desire is not just for yourself, but also that others would have the same walk.

What you do does not determine who you are, but who you are should determine what you do.

Right after I graduated from college, I secured my first real job with a set salary—about $12,000 more than I asked for—and benefits. I'll never forget being in my apartment complex parking lot, blubbering on and on to my mama about getting this job and how much money they had offered me.

My boss called me and gave me a title, a name, for my position. He gave me a purpose and an objective. He told me when I should be at work and what I was supposed to do. He *called* me.

Salvation does not come absent of responsibility.

That is similar to how God calls us, with one exception. When God calls us, it starts with the relationship, our walk with Him, and this depends heavily on our position before Him, which must be one of self-denial. This leads to our responsibility, our work for Him in response to what He has done for us and for others. It is so important to remember that your call to identity is also a call to responsibility.

> Therefore, if anyone is in Christ, he is a new creation. The old has passed away; behold, the new has come. All this is from God, who through Christ reconciled us to himself and gave us the ministry of reconciliation; that is, in Christ God was reconciling the world to himself, not counting their trespasses against them, and entrusting to us the message of reconciliation. Therefore, we are ambassadors for Christ, God making his appeal through us. We implore you on behalf of Christ, be reconciled to God.
> **—2 Corinthians 5:17–20** (ESV)

What you do does not determine who you are, but who you are should determine what you do. When we become followers of Christ, we accept the responsibility to do the work of reconciliation as messengers of the gospel and ambassadors for Christ. This is not a request; it is a command. It is the foundation of your calling as a believer. Salvation does not come absent of responsibility.

The First Call: To Deny

> *After paying the fare....*
> —*Jonah 1:3 (NIV)*

Perhaps you've been on the phone when another call came in, and you had to decide whether to continue with the first call or take the second one. To answer one call often means to deny another.

Jonah had two calls, either to obey God or to deny Him. When you answer one call, you deny something else. When you answer the call of your flesh, you are denying Christ. What you *choose* to do often reveals what you *don't want* to do. A commitment to one thing is a communication to the other. What are you communicating to God with your decisions?

I used to refuse to be around people who were "too healthy" because they always wanted to tell me how unhealthy my food was. My aunt is very health-conscious. She's a beautiful woman in her early seventies, and you would never guess her age because she eats clean and takes care of herself. I lived with her and my uncle for a time. Every night, she would cook a wholesome dinner, and I would bring in junk food. I had a few health complications at the time, and she would ask about what I was eating and if it was good for me. I said to myself, "Listen, I'm going to eat somewhere else if you keep lecturing me. Just because you don't want it doesn't mean I have to give it up."

"Ryan," she would tell me, "your desire for that kind of food tells me that you are denying yourself the opportunity to be healthy." She was right, as always!

It costs you to do the right thing, and it costs you to do the wrong thing. Either way, you have to pay.

Are you denying God's call by the calls that you answer? Are you saying, "God, lost people are not important to me," because you don't want to share your faith? Are you telling Him that what He did on Calvary's cross is not as important as what you want to talk about, your reputation, or being politically correct?

Jonah had to make a decision. He had an opportunity to do what God called him to do, and he ran the other way. The Bible says that he went to Joppa, where he boarded a ship bound for Tarshish—note this—"after paying the fare" (Jonah 1:3 NIV).

Every call costs you something. It costs you to do the right thing, and it costs you to do the wrong thing. Either way, you have to pay. You have to make a sacrifice on one end or the other.

Jonah paid a literal price to get away from the call of God. It's the microeconomics principle of opportunity cost: putting time, energy, and effort into one thing costs the opportunity for doing something else.

The reality is that answering God's call on your life is going to cost you something. You're going to have to make the sacrifice. You're going to have to deny yourself. But guess what? *Not* answering God's call on your life is going to cost you as well, and oftentimes it will cost you more.

I used to work in sales, and I would frequently ask people when they were trying to make a decision, "Are you more interested in quality or in getting something cost effective?" ("Cost effective" is code for "cheap," but that's not a word you use in sales!) You've heard before that you're going to pay either on the front end or on the back end, and that's true in our walk with God as well. If we do what He tells us to do when He tells us to do it, it will cost far less than if we choose disobedience.

Someone asked me recently what it was about my wife that made me decide to marry her. When we were dating, she went away to a conference to sing and minister, and I couldn't go because I had to preach somewhere else. She was gone for three days. *Three days.* You would have thought from talking to me during that time that she had moved across the country. I thought that I was going to lose my mind, that I surely would not make it but for the grace of God. While I knew that it would cost me to be with her, I came to see during that separation that it would cost me even more to be without her. I answered the call and put a ring on it!

You cannot have commitment without denial of self. To commit to something or to someone, you must deny yourself something or someone else. How are you doing when it comes to denying?

Consider Jonah. As we have seen, Jonah was a prophet of Israel who ministered between 800 and 750 BC while

King Jeroboam II was in power. Jeroboam had brought peace to the land by restoring traditional borders, ending almost 100 years of conflict between Israel and Syria.

*And since the L*ORD *had not said he would blot out the name of Israel from under heaven, he saved them by the hand of Jeroboam son of Jehoash.*

As for the other events of Jeroboam's reign, all he did, and his military achievements, including how he recovered for Israel both Damascus and Hamath, which had belonged to Judah, are they not written in the book of the annals of the kings of Israel?
—2 Kings 14:27–28 *(NIV)*

As a result, King Jeroboam and his people were enjoying prosperity economically, politically, and militarily (2 Kings 14:23–15:7; 2 Chronicles 26). Life for Israel seemed to be going well at the time when God said to Jonah, "I need you to go to this evil city called Nineveh."

"Wait, hold up, Lord. No, no, I'm good doing what I am doing. Everything is going well. I don't want a challenge! Lord, I already did this, this and that. Did You see? I thought You were going to put me in this other ministry here. No, no, no." Jonah would have to deny himself to go to Nineveh; his was a call out of comfort.

Centuries later, Jesus the Messiah would teach on this very concept:

Then he said to them all: "Whoever wants to be my disciple must deny themselves and take up their cross daily and

follow me. For whoever wants to save their life will lose it,
but whoever loses their life for me will save it."
—**Luke 9:23–24** *(NIV)*

This is a choice on your part. Jesus says that anyone can follow Him, but you must be willing to pay the cost, to answer the call of God on your life and take up your cross daily. That cross is not something you carry around to show people and say, "Hey, this is what I'm doing!" Rather, it is a burden that costs you something every day in commitment and self-denial. Only after you have denied yourself and taken up your cross does Jesus add, "Follow Me." Until you are ready to deny yourself, you are not ready to follow.

You don't know the cost until you answer the call. If I had known the stuff I was going to go through when God called me into ministry and later to plant Vertical Church, I might not have answered the call.

My wife and I went to premarital counseling, received great information, and read some excellent books on marriage, but nobody could tell us the cost of building a strong and healthy marriage. Every call has a cost. It's going to cost you to follow God, but it will also cost you not to follow Him.

The Second Call: To Walk

But Jonah ran away from the LORD and headed for Tarshish.

—**Jonah 1:3** *(NIV)*

The second call is a call to walk with Him, to follow Jesus. In *The Message* version of Matthew 11:29–30, Jesus said, "Walk with me and work with me—watch how I do it. Learn the unforced rhythms of grace. I won't lay anything heavy or ill-fitting on you. Keep company with me and you'll learn to live freely and lightly" (MSG).

A lot of times, we skip this portion of our calling because we focus on a specific task or title. But our relationship with God, our walk with God, is the fuel for our work. God wants you to be with Him more than He wants you to work for Him.

Maybe you are goal-oriented like I am. I want to achieve things, and I want to acquire. But my walk always fuels my work. Without the walk, I lose favor, I lose the anointing, and I lose grace for the work. Whenever you see God calling someone to a new thing, there is always a relationship established prior to the work.

In the Bible, when God wanted to describe someone who was intimate with Him, He said that person walked with Him:

> *Altogether, Enoch lived a total of 365 years. Enoch walked faithfully with God; then he was no more, because God took him away.*
> *—Genesis 5:23–24 (NIV)*

> *Noah was a righteous man, blameless in his generation. Noah walked with God.*
> *—Genesis 6:9 (ESV)*

> *Then he blessed Joseph and said, "May the God before whom my fathers Abraham and Isaac walked faithfully, the God who has been my shepherd all my life to this day..."*
> **—Genesis 48:15** (NIV)

> *I will also walk among you and be your God, and you shall be My people.*
> **—Leviticus 26:12** (NASB)

Enoch walked with God. Noah walked with God. Abraham and Isaac walked with God. God told the children of Israel that He would walk among them.

Is this for only a select few? Not at all! God desires all His children be in intimate relationship with Him. God said in Deuteronomy 8:6 that we show we are observing His commands "by walking in his ways and by fearing him" (ESV). Micah 6:8 says, "And what does the LORD require of you? To act justly and to love mercy and to walk humbly with your God" (NIV).

What exactly does it mean to walk with God? To help answer the question, let's look at Enoch's walk with God:

> *By faith Enoch was taken up so that he would not see death; AND HE WAS NOT FOUND BECAUSE GOD TOOK HIM UP; for he obtained the witness that before his being taken up he was pleasing to God. And without faith it is impossible to please Him, for he who comes to God must believe that He is and that He is a rewarder of those who seek Him.*
> **—Hebrews 11:5–6** (NASB)

Before Enoch was taken away from the people who wanted to hurt him because of his righteous life, he pleased God. What does it mean to please God? Verse 6 answers that question: "Without faith it is impossible to please Him, for he who comes to God must believe that He is…" (Hebrews 11:6 NASB).

Enoch believed what God said about the things he couldn't see or understand. Noah did the same when he prepared the ark for the salvation of his household. Those who believe and obey God have a special, intimate relationship with Him. They believe Him, and they walk *with* Him.

Conversely, notice how Jonah responded when God called him to go to Nineveh:

> But Jonah ran away from the LORD and headed for Tarshish. He went down to Joppa, where he found a ship bound for that port. After paying the fare, he went aboard and sailed for Tarshish to flee from the LORD.
> *—Jonah 1:3 (NIV)*

Jonah made a decision to walk *away* from God. The New American Standard version describes this turning from God as fleeing "from the presence of the LORD" (Jonah 1:3 NASB). If God is everywhere, how does a person walk away from His presence?

God gave a word, and Jonah chose to walk away from the opportunity to be obedient to that word. He didn't walk away and leave God somewhere, but he turned his back on the presence of God. He disobeyed God's instruction and did not trust God for what he could not see—or didn't want to see.

We, too, can become concerned about our work while giving no thought to our walk. We grow frustrated in our work for God and wonder, "Why isn't my work working?" And God answers, "Because you are not walking with Me."

One of the greatest truths revealed to me is that God did not send His Son to die on a cross so that I could work for Him, but so that I could walk with Him. Jesus came to restore relationship. Walking with God has always been the priority. Many times we deny the walk in the name of the work.

Every single day, you need to ask yourself, "Am I walking with God? Am I trusting Him?" Do you start your day walking with Him, or do you go to Him with your to-do list? Do you spend time in prayer and meditation on who He is and find out His priorities for your day? Do you then trust Him to carry out what He is calling you to do?

I believe that it's your walk that will bless your work, not your work that will bless your walk. When you walk with God and still have joy in the midst of sorrow and peace in the midst of turmoil, others will say, "I want that. I don't know what that is, but I want it."

My young son Wesley constantly wants to play games on the iPad, and he also wants to follow me everywhere. Recently we were at home, and every time I stood up to walk to the next room, Wesley would cry, "Don't leave me!" He would pick up his iPad and try to play games on it while following me from room to room.

"Watch out!" I told him. "There's a wall there, and it's not going to move." But he was absorbed in his iPad and still trying to follow me, so he ended up running into a wall anyway. He came to me, crying, and I tried to explain, "If you would just look at me and listen to me, you wouldn't run into the walls, son."

Sometimes our hands are so full with the work that we fail in the walk. Then we cry out, "Lord, why did I run into this situation?" We ran into it because we were too focused on what was in our hands and what we wanted to do. Before we load up with our stuff each day, we should ask, "Lord, where are *You* going? I just want to walk with You."

Later Wesley and I were downstairs, and he was trying to follow me upstairs. About halfway up the steps, he said, "If I just give you the iPad, you can carry me, and we will get up there at the same time."

Most Christians are running into walls all over the place. I don't believe that God makes us busy; we make ourselves busy. I've never known God to overwhelm His saints; we get ourselves overwhelmed. If you learn to take what's in your hands and put it in God's hands and then let God carry you, you will get there when He gets there.

The Third Call: To the Lost

Go to the great city of Nineveh and preach against it, because its wickedness has come up before me.
—Jonah 1:2 (NIV)

God called Jonah to go and preach against wicked Nineveh, whose people were lost and far from God.

Reaching the lost is the work of those who walk with
Christ.

*It is for this call—to be witnesses of Christ
to a lost world—that we receive power.*

When our church-planting team was meeting together
to try to cast a vision to let people know about the new
church, the Lord continued to put Acts 1:8 in my heart. I
shared on this verse for months: "But you will receive
power when the Holy Spirit comes on you; and you will
be my witnesses in Jerusalem, and in all Judea and Sa-
maria, and to the ends of the earth" (Acts 1:8 NIV).

It is for this call—to be witnesses of Christ to a lost
world—that we receive power. We have power to reach,
to go out into all the earth, and to testify about Him—not
just as witnesses, but as *His* witnesses. What does a witness do? A witness tells what happened. That's all you
have to do. That's your job description. I love the words
of John Wesley: "You have nothing to do but to save
souls. Therefore, spend and be spent in this work."[1]

*He doesn't call us to the work, hoping that
we will walk with Him. No, He calls us to the
walk so we can do the work.*

What do I tell? Tell them what is happening while you are on the walk. But if you have no walk, you have no witness. This is why it's imperative to focus on your walk. When you walk with Him, you will see what He can do, you will see His power, you will see His work through your life, and then you can be a witness to the ends of the earth. He doesn't call us to the work, hoping that we will walk with Him. No, He calls us to the walk so we can do the work.

God called Jonah to walk in obedience to His commands, to go to Nineveh and call the people who were engulfed in sin and wickedness to repent. However, Jonah was not walking intimately with God, and he turned from Him.

When somebody tells me, "I don't know if I can do that," I understand. I just pray for that person's walk. I could tell you why you should do something, but if you don't have the walk to encourage and inspire you, you won't have the power to do the work. This is why the disciples had to walk with Jesus for three years before their ministry began. John Newton said it this way: "Christ has taken our nature into heaven to represent us; and has left us on earth, with His nature, to represent Him."[2]

The call on your life leads you into relationship with God, which impacts others who are "without hope and without God in the world" (Ephesians 2:12 NIV). Souls are on the line. It's our mission to reach those who are far from God and bring them back to Him through a vertical relationship with Jesus Christ.

God doesn't need more people to do His work; He wants more people to walk with Him. When people walk with Him, they will do the work! Your work is a reflection of your walk. Every single day I walk with Him, I know how much He has blessed me. I see His grace and mercy made new every morning, and it makes me *want* to tell somebody that Jesus still lives. It makes me *want* to answer the call.

WORKBOOK

Chapter One Questions

Question: What call has God placed on your life? How have you responded?

_____

_____

_____

_____

_____

_____

_____

_____

_____

_____

Question: In what ways might you be prioritizing your own desires over God's call? What is one change you can make today to place God's priorities first?

_____

_____

_____

_____

_____

_____

_____

_____

_____

_____

Question: How do you pursue a walk with God on a daily basis? What is one specific step you will take to grow in your relationship with Him?

_____

_____

_____

_____

_____

_____

_____

_____

_____

_____

_____

Action: Be mindful of which call on your life you're answering and how you're answering it. Respond to God's call on your heart by embracing your true identity, destiny, and responsibilities. Decide how to pursue an intimate relationship with Him and His Word on a daily basis.

Ask God to help you listen for what He is truly telling you instead of what your desires are telling you. Instead of denying Him, deny yourself. Then walk with Him and reach out to the lost!

Chapter One Notes

_____

_____

_____

_____

_____

_____

_____

_____

_____

_____

_____

_____

_____

_____

_____

_____

_____

_____

_____

_____

CHAPTER TWO

The Purpose of the Call:
God Calls You for Others

*Then the LORD sent a great wind on the sea, and such a vi-
olent storm arose that the ship threatened to break up. All
the sailors were afraid and each cried out to his own god.
And they threw the cargo into the sea to lighten the ship.*
—Jonah 1:4–5 *(NIV)*

When I began my job in car sales, my supervisors told
me all the time not to take personal calls on the floor. If a
call had nothing to do with my responsibilities as a sales-
man, then I was not to take it during business hours.

God's call on your life is different because it is both
personal—what you are called to do—and business—the
work of the kingdom. The call on you as an individual is
directly correlated with the responsibility God has given
to the entire body of Christ.

Jonah was a prophet of the Lord, which meant that his
job was to speak on behalf of God, to be His representative and His voice. In the midst of a successful ministry,

God called Jonah to do a specific thing, just as He calls each of us. He asked Jonah to go to an evil place where people were rejecting God and preach to them a message of judgment. He asked Jonah to leave his place of comfort out of obedience, even though he didn't agree with what God was telling him to do.

A call is not just for the church or the pastor. God's call is for each believer to reach out and make disciples. This plan to share the good news of Jesus Christ is found in what is known as the Great Commission (Matthew 28:18–20).

This is the personal responsibility of each one of us. It's your job. This isn't like in the workplace, where you have the option of saying, "That's not in my job description." No. When it comes to telling people that Jesus lived, that He died on the cross for the sins of the world, that God raised Him from the dead, and that people have access to God through Jesus Christ and Jesus Christ alone, guess what? It's your job. It's both a call for the church and a personal call.

Your call doesn't just *impact* others; your call is always *for* others. God's purpose for your life is not for you to be great, but for you to help somebody else. Fruit trees don't eat fruit. The fruit of your salvation, redemption, and restoration is not just for you, but for others as well. Whatever you produce in your life is not for yourself; it's for somebody else.

Sleeping Through the Storm

Jonah ran defiantly from the presence of the Lord, hopping on a boat and fleeing from Joppa (about thirty miles northwest of Jerusalem) in the direction of Tarshish, the most distant city in the known world at the time. Tarshish was 2,200 miles west of Joppa, on the edge of Spain. But Jonah didn't make it to Tarshish because God caused a great storm to develop on the sea. The storm was so violent that the ship was about to fall apart.

There are two other instances in the Bible that describe a storm this way. One was when Jesus and His disciples were trying to cross over the Sea of Galilee:

That day when evening came, he said to his disciples, "Let us go over to the other side." Leaving the crowd behind, they took him along, just as he was, in the boat. There were also other boats with him. A furious squall came up, and the waves broke over the boat, so that it was nearly swamped. Jesus was in the stern, sleeping on a cushion. The disciples woke him and said to him, "Teacher, don't you care if we drown?"
—Mark 4:35–38 *(NIV)*

The other was when Paul was traveling to Rome. This storm was so severe that his ship broke up, and he floated to shore on pieces of wreckage.

Before very long, a wind of hurricane force, called the Northeaster, swept down from the island. The ship was caught by the storm and could not head into the wind; so we gave way to it and were driven along. As we passed to the lee of a small island called Cauda, we were hardly able to make the lifeboat secure, so the men hoisted it aboard. Then they passed ropes under the ship itself to hold it together. Because they were afraid they would run aground on the sandbars of Syrtis, they lowered the sea anchor and let the ship be driven along. We took such a violent battering from the storm that the next day they began to throw the cargo overboard. On the third day, they threw the ship's tackle overboard with their own hands. When neither sun nor stars appeared for many days and the storm continued raging, we finally gave up all hope of being saved.

—Acts 27:14–20 (NIV)

Why are these examples of violent storms significant? God can calm storms, but it's important to remember that God can also stir up a storm. In each of these situations, the expert mariners, who were prepared and equipped to handle intense storms, were impacted by a storm so great that it terrified them. They had no hope but God. In each situation, the sailors had not done anything wrong. The storm simply rose up! But God was using the storm to teach something deeper.

In Jonah's case, the issue was his defiant heart. God would use the storm to humble Jonah, but the sailors were also affected. Sometimes the storm God uses to transform one person directly impacts others.

Jonah 1:4 says that "the LORD sent a great wind on the sea" (NIV). Some people think that every time something comes against them, it's from the enemy. No. Who sent this storm? The Lord sent it in response to Jonah's hardened heart. However, it was not intended to punish him, but to redirect his heart toward Nineveh. We will see more of this later.

Our Disobedience Impacts Others

The captain went to him and said, "How can you sleep? Get up and call on your god! Maybe he will take notice of us so that we will not perish."

—**Jonah 1:6** *(NIV)*

All the mariners on Jonah's ship were impacted by the storm because of Jonah's disobedience. First, they threw cargo overboard. When that didn't work, "each cried out to his own god" (Jonah 1:5 NIV)—a typical response when man does his best to fix an unfixable problem. Sometimes you don't want to think that the things happening on your ship have anything to do with you. But Jonah's disobedience to God impacted every other person on that boat.

> *Your personal call always has a public impact.*

There were different types of people on this ship, with varying religions and beliefs. When the Bible says that they cried out to their gods, it doesn't mean *the* God, Yahweh. God used Jonah, even in his disobedience, to introduce them to the one and only living God. Ironically, a pagan captain told Jonah to call on his God, rebuking him for the situation. "Call on your god!" he urged.

Who on your ship is believing in another god? Who on your ship is trying to figure out a way through this storm called life by human effort? Jonah knew the one true God, yet his behavior and defiance did not reflect God to the lost sailors. He slept while putting others in danger.

Who in your life doesn't know the true God? Your personal call always has a public impact. When you do what God has called you to do, you impact others publicly. When you don't do what God has called you to do, that also has an impact beyond yourself.

*You were not born into **your** world; you were born into **the** world.*

A lot of times, we are just stuck in our own little worlds, and we make decisions based on what we want, what we think and feel is right, and how something impacts us. Always remember that life is bigger than *your* life. You were not born into *your* world; you were born into *the* world.

When Jonah got on the ship, he was only thinking about himself. Because of his self-centeredness, the people on his ship went through a storm. While they were trying every tactic, every superstition, every religious ritual they could think of, where was Jonah?

But Jonah had gone below deck, where he lay down and fell into a deep sleep. The captain went to him and said, "How can you sleep? Get up and call on your god! Maybe he will take notice of us so that we will not perish."
—Jonah 1:5–6 (NIV)

What a question! "How can you sleep?" In a world full of darkness and brokenness, can you hear God asking you that same question as you read this book? Jonah was sleeping, even as his disobedience placed the rest of the people on the ship in mortal danger!

Jonah, the Sailors' Source of Trouble

> *And they said to one another, "Come, let us cast lots, that we may know for whose cause this trouble has come upon us." So they cast lots, and the lot fell on Jonah. Then they said to him, "Please tell us! For whose cause is this trouble upon us? What is your occupation? And where do you come from? What is your country? And of what people are you?"*
> *—Jonah 1:7–8 (NKJV)*

The sailors prayed to their gods to no avail. They were terrified as the storm worsened. So they searched through the ship, trying to find the person responsible for this storm. When you don't answer the call of God on your life, someone else's prayer goes unanswered. When you don't answer God's call, there's a problem going unsolved. But when you choose to obey God's call on your life, you become the answer to somebody else's prayer.

What motivated the sailors to think that the storm was sent because one of them had wronged his god? Was it superstition? We can't know for sure, but the act of casting lots indicated their belief in something supernatural. The lot fell to Jonah, and the sailors began to drill him, searching for answers. What was his occupation? He was a prophet. This likely terrified the sailors even more!

Jonah answered them, "I am a Hebrew and I worship the LORD, the God of heaven, who made the sea and the dry land" (Jonah 1:9 NIV). The gig was up. The sailors shared a ship with an Israelite, and they were afraid of this man who had fled his own God. The sailors exclaimed, "What have you done?" (Jonah 1:10 NIV). Even unbelievers understand some things about God.

Jonah asked to be thrown into the sea, hoping that would solve the problem and calm the storm (Jonah 1:12). The sailors knew that if they kept Jonah on the ship, they would perish. But if they tossed him overboard, they would be guilty of killing an innocent man and would face the wrath of Jonah's God!

A Spiritual Wake-Up Call

Remember that while everyone else panicked, Jonah was asleep in the bottom of the boat. You should never let your sleep be at the expense of another's suffering! If you're comatose when it comes to the call of God on your life, the people around you may be going through turmoil and suffering because you failed to answer the call. If people choose not to hear what you say about Jesus, that's fine. Just don't let it be because you were sleeping.

On Saturday mornings, when my wife and I are hoping that everyone will sleep in, little Wesley, who didn't want to get up Monday through Friday, often calls out about 6 a.m., "Daddy! I want fuffins." (My son says "fuffins" because he can't pronounce the *m* in "muffins" yet.) Wesley ensures that his parents wake up from *our* sleep so we can stop *his* suffering. Wesley is saying, in effect, "Daddy, you can't sleep because if you sleep, I suffer. You know what I need, and you know I can't get it by myself."

People like to sleep. Sleeping feels good. It's comforting and beneficial to you, but you can't do it all the time. As a Christian, it's critical to stay awake and alert, especially when God has placed a call on your life.

I've had times when I needed the people around me to wake up and help me. I needed them to care enough about me to see not what I did, but where I was going. I needed mature believers to help me have authentic relationships within the body of Christ.

There are people in your life who don't serve the same God you serve. While you are sleeping, a sinful situation may be creating a storm in their lives and causing them to suffer. They need you to wake up and share your Savior. It's not that you're not alert physically, but you may be spiritually asleep and unaware of the things going on around you.

There are people in our communities and even in our families struggling to fix their lives because we are sleeping. In fact, there may be someone who's praying right now for God's deliverance through somebody just like you. But when you make excuses—"God, I am not worthy. God, I am not good enough. I've made too many mistakes. God, I don't do the right things. God, I don't know enough scriptures. God, I don't go to church enough"—then the person who needs you must continue to wait and repeat the same prayer over and over because you're refusing to answer the call!

Jonah, Wake Up!

The captain of the ship begged Jonah to wake up. God had called Jonah to go rebuke Nineveh, and now this foreigner, this unbelieving Gentile, rebuked him. After the sailors cast lots and found out who was to blame for the storm, they asked Jonah, "Listen, who are you and what are you doing?"

It's kind of like when your phone is ringing in a public environment, and everybody hears it but you. Everyone watches and listens as you ignore your ringing phone. Maybe the caller calls a second time, and everyone around you is wondering why you don't just answer the phone.

The sailors knew that Jonah was supposed to be doing something other than sleeping, and they wanted to know what that was. If you are not busy doing what God has called you to do, then what are you doing?

The apostle Paul asked an interesting question to remind Christians about what we are supposed to be doing:

> ...for, "Everyone who calls on the name of the Lord will be saved." How, then, can they call on the one they have not believed in? And how can they believe in the one of whom they have not heard? And how can they hear without someone preaching to them?
> —*Romans 10:13-14 (NIV)*

How will the world know Jesus if Christians are asleep? You go to work and put a smile on your face, you've got a bumper sticker on your car, you've got the cross as the screensaver on your computer, and you've got thirty thousand wristbands that say everything you should be saying with your mouth. But how will they *hear* if you are still asleep?

The Message translation puts it like this:

> But how can people call for help if they don't know who to trust? And how can they know who to trust if they haven't heard of the One who can be trusted? And how can they hear if nobody tells them? And how is anyone going to tell them, unless someone is sent to do it?
>
> —**Romans 10:14** (MSG)

The world wants to know: What are you doing? Who are you? Where are you from? What are you about? Are you just coming together on Sunday mornings in your fancy buildings with your lights, your singers, and your band and doing a little thing for an hour and a half and then going home? Is that all you are doing?

How is the world going to know about Jesus Christ if we don't tell them?

More Than Sacrifice

> [Jonah] answered, "I am a Hebrew and I worship the LORD, the God of heaven, who made the sea and the dry land."
>
> This terrified them and they asked, "What have you done?" (They knew he was running away from the LORD, because he had already told them so.)
>
> The sea was getting rougher and rougher. So they asked him, "What should we do to you to make the sea calm down for us?"

"Pick me up and throw me into the sea," he replied, "and it will become calm. I know that it is my fault that this great storm has come upon you."

—Jonah 1:9–12 (NIV)

Jonah finally fessed up that he was the problem, the cause of the terrible storm. He not only admitted his guilt, but even denied himself and surrendered to the sailors. Jonah didn't jump out of the ship on his own, but he told the sailors that they should toss him overboard. The sea was growing more and more violent, and perhaps Jonah knew that God alone would protect him and the sailors.

Waving the white flag of surrender is not merely giving up. It's also saying, "I am giving myself over to Your control."

Surrender is a huge part of what it means to be a follower of Christ. In Chapter One, we talked about denying yourself. However, if you are to answer the call, you must move from sacrifice, or denial, to surrender. Sacrifice says, "I give it up," but surrender says, "I will pick it up." Sacrifice says, "I will let go of what I have," but surrender picks up another's burden.

Waving the white flag of surrender is not merely giving up. It's also saying, "I am giving myself over to Your control." Giving is one thing, but surrender says, "Lord, do what You want to do with me." If you want to follow Christ, realize that it's not only giving up what you want to do, but also picking up what God wants to do in your life.

When the sailors did what Jonah asked and threw him into the sea, the storm immediately calmed (Jonah 1:15). Jonah's God was real, and his surrender resulted in salvation for many. Scripture says that the sailors "feared the LORD exceedingly, and they offered a sacrifice to the LORD and made vows" (Jonah 1:16 ESV).

One surrender results in multiple salvations. Ask the Lord, "What do You want to do with my life?" If that is too big to think about, ask Him, "What do You want to do with my day? Lord, whom do You want me to help today?"

The Sailors' First Response

> "Pick me up and throw me into the sea," he replied, "and it will become calm. I know that it is my fault that this great storm has come upon you."
>
> Instead, the men did their best to row back to land.
> **—Jonah 1:12–13** (NIV)

Notice in the above verses that the sailors wanted salvation without sacrifice. They heard what Jonah said, but they kept trying it their own way, rowing even harder. Man will always try to figure out a way to save himself, but like the sailors' attempts, it will always come to naught.

The Sailors' Second Response

Jonah 1:13 concludes: "But they could not, for the sea grew even wilder than before" (NIV). The sailors had to reach the point of understanding that nothing they could do would save them. They needed the God of Abraham, Isaac, and Jacob to rescue them from impending death!

No matter how hard people try, they won't get to God without Jesus. No matter how much effort a person exerts, it cannot save. No self-help book can save. Without Jesus Christ, no person can experience the joy of the Lord, peace beyond understanding, or salvation everlasting. Salvation comes from God alone: "For it is by grace you have been saved, through faith—and this is not from yourselves, it is the gift of God—not by works, so that no one can boast" (Ephesians 2:8–9 NIV).

Tucked away in the brief book of Jonah is the gospel of salvation:

> Then they cried out to the LORD, "Please, LORD, do not let us die for taking this man's life. Do not hold us accountable for killing an innocent man, for you, LORD, have done as you pleased." Then they took Jonah and threw him overboard, and the raging sea grew calm. At this the men greatly feared the LORD, and they offered a sacrifice to the LORD and made vows to him.
>
> *—Jonah 1:14–16 (NIV)*

God alone saves. As we see in Jonah, this message is not new in the New Testament; in fact, it is as old as time. The psalmist wrote, "Our God is a God who saves; from the Sovereign LORD comes escape from death" (Psalm

68:20 NIV). Isaiah wrote, "Behold, God is my salvation; I will trust, and will not be afraid" (Isaiah 12:2 ESV).

Jonah's life, once he was obedient, foreshadowed Jesus. The difference is that Jonah initially said *no* to the will of God, and Jesus always said *yes*. Jesus came into this world, onto our ship. These mariners, with their varying beliefs and gods, were in a storm of judgment. Jonah told them to hurl him into the sea. His surrender foreshadowed what Jesus did for humanity on the cross.

Like Jonah, Christ gave His life not for His own salvation, but for the salvation of others. Jonah's story teaches Christians that surrendering our one life can result in multiple salvations. Jesus Christ surrendered Himself, dying not for one or for twelve, but for all mankind. I am so thankful today that Jesus Christ answered the call!

Your sacrifice, your surrender, is not just for you. And it's not to have more people to do work, but that more people would know the heavenly Father.

WORKBOOK

Chapter Two Questions

Question: How might your disobedience toward God, past or present, have impacted others?

_____

_____

_____

_____

_____

_____

_____

_____

_____

_____

_____

Question: What are you holding back from God today? How can you surrender your life and desires more completely to Him?

_____

_____

_____

_____

_____

_____

_____

_____

_____

_____

Action: To answer the call, you have to wake up! Your salvation and the salvation of others depend on it. Avoid inaction and disobedience, which can lead to real suffering and lasting harm for you and other people. Remember that salvation isn't about doing what you feel like doing; it requires surrender and sacrifice.

Ask God to show you those areas of your life that you haven't surrendered to Him. Where are you struggling? Remember to be honest with Him because He knows you better than you know yourself!

Chapter Two Notes

CHAPTER THREE

Remember, Realign, and Respond to the Call:
Perspective Determines Posture

Now the LORD provided a huge fish to swallow Jonah, and Jonah was in the belly of the fish three days and three nights.
—Jonah 1:17 (NIV)

When I heard this story as a kid and saw the drawings of Jonah inside a fish, I had a hard time believing that such a thing could really happen. I'd never seen a fish large enough for a person to fit inside. When researching this possibility later on, I learned that similar stories are found around the world. Certain species of sharks and whales tend to swallow their food whole, along with enormous quantities of water.[3] Sailors have reportedly caught these great fish and cut them open to find a human being still alive inside.[4]

Fact or fiction? Personally, I swim in pools, maybe a lake or a pond, but I steer wide of any body of water that boasts fish large enough to swallow me!

> From inside the fish Jonah prayed to the LORD his God.
> —*Jonah 2:1* (NIV)

My first thought on reading this scripture was: "You know, it might be a bit late to be praying, Jonah. Didn't God already ask you to go to Nineveh? And *now* you want to pray?"

I've had times in my life when God asked me to do something. I knew what the Word of God said and what I was supposed to do, yet it wasn't until I sank into a dark place that I said, "Okay, Lord, maybe I will go to church. Maybe I will pray. Maybe I will open up the Bible."

If your fear is greater than your motivation, you will not move. But if you are going to tell people about Jesus Christ, the very first thing you must always remember is where you were before you were walking with Him.

The Depths

Jonah painted an incredible picture in chapter 2 of what finally motivated him to do what he did not want to do:

> He said: "In my distress I called to the LORD, and he answered me. From deep in the realm of the dead I called for help, and you listened to my cry. You hurled me into the depths, into the very heart of the seas, and the currents swirled about me; all your waves and breakers swept over

me. I said, 'I have been banished from your sight; yet I will look again toward your holy temple.' The engulfing waters threatened me, the deep surrounded me; seaweed was wrapped around my head. To the roots of the mountains I sank down; the earth beneath barred me in forever. But you, LORD my God, brought my life up from the pit."
—Jonah 2:2–6 *(NIV)*

After an experience like Jonah had, wouldn't you want to share? Wouldn't you want to tell somebody about that kind of God? It's my personal walk that moves me to share my faith. It's not what God did for *you*, but what God did for *me* that makes me want to tell people that Jesus lives.

I am the only one who can remember when I was in a stressful, dark place. It's this memory that makes me want to tell people, "If God could hear my cry, He will hear your cry." But if I forget where I was before I met Christ, if I don't keep that before me, then sometimes I forget that I need to tell people about God.

Jonah remembered, and he described that dark place: "You hurled me into the depths, into the very heart of the seas, and the currents swirled about me; all your waves and breakers swept over me" (Jonah 2:3 NIV). The King James Version says, "…all thy billows and thy waves passed over me" (Jonah 2:3 KJV). The psalmist was remembering, too, when he wrote: "He lifted me out of the slimy pit, out of the mud and mire; he set my feet on a rock and gave me a firm place to stand" (Psalm 40:2 NIV). Praising God, this songwriter recalled the dark pit, but he also recounted God's salvation and how He set his feet on solid ground.

I have no idea how people live without Jesus Christ. I don't know what I was thinking before I had a genuine relationship with Him. Jonah painted a picture in his prayer of how frustrating life can be without the Lord. He described the danger.

Unlike Jonah, most people don't look like they are in danger. Sometimes you cannot see depression on people. You cannot see confusion in someone's life or the lack of peace in someone's heart. You can't always see frustration or loneliness.

This is why I tell the servant leaders at church that every Sunday we've got to minister as if it's someone's last Sunday on earth. We don't know who is coming into the church saying, "If nothing happens for me today, I am taking my life." Every Sunday a prodigal son may be coming home or walking away forever, but you often can't see people's internal struggles or the danger they are in.

Don't Wait Any Longer

This is why there is urgency when it comes to sharing our faith. Often you can't see the billows and the waves crashing in on people because they come to work, they smile, they do their job, and they go home. Someone may appear to have the picture-perfect life, but you don't know what's going on in the heart. People who don't have Jesus in their hearts are in danger.

In verse 4, Jonah made a powerful statement: "I have been banished from your sight" (Jonah 2:4 NIV). He was talking about how he felt when he was thrown overboard. Banishment does not mean simply going outside. It's not even like what my grandma used to say: "You all go outside and don't come back in this house till dark!" Banishment means, "Go outside and don't ever come back." It is the Hebrew word *garash*, which means "to drive out, expel, cast out, divorce, or thrust away."[5] Jonah felt as if he'd been thrown away; he was unwanted and unloved.

> *People who don't have Jesus in their hearts are in danger.*

However, in the midst of this brokenness, knowing that he deserved this suffering, Jonah declared, "Nevertheless I will look again toward Your holy temple" (Jonah 2:4 NASB). Looking toward God's holy temple means acknowledging God and choosing to focus on Him.

Then Jonah stated:

> *The engulfing waters threatened me, the deep surrounded me; seaweed was wrapped around my head. To the roots of the mountains I sank down; the earth beneath barred me in forever.*
> *—Jonah 2:5–6 (NIV)*

Forget any childhood imagery of Jonah treading water or doing the backstroke at the top of the sea while a big fish pops up for a snack. Jonah went down "to the roots of the mountain," meaning the floor of the ocean.

Have you ever felt barred in by your own sin? Maybe you felt trapped by your past. Jonah knew that in his own strength, he could not get out. If you don't remember a time when you were barred in and trapped, then when you see someone else in that state, you likely won't be moved to tell that person about Jesus, who set you free.

Jonah was able to recall how God saved him:

> But you, LORD my God, brought my life up from the pit.
>
> When my life was ebbing away, I remembered you, LORD, and my prayer rose to you, to your holy temple.
>
> Those who cling to worthless idols turn away from God's love for them.
>
> —*Jonah 2:6–8 (NIV)*

In the same way, we must not forget how God brought us from a place of death and separation from Him to life. The great fish that swallowed up Jonah was not his punishment, but his rescue. It was the rescue that Jonah needed to remind him of the power of God.

We've All Been There

My middle son was recently asking me about the Ten Commandments. One of his friends told him that because of Jesus' grace, the Ten Commandments don't apply to us anymore.

I said, "No, son, Jesus actually expects more of us. Jesus explained that while the law says, 'Do not commit adultery,' now if you look with lust, you are committing adultery in your heart. Son, it's not just what you *do* now, but also what you *think*. You are just as guilty to think it as someone else is to do it."

You've got to remember not just what you used to do, but also how you used to think. If you don't remember those thoughts, those feelings, those emotions, those bad decisions, then when you see people whose thinking is all wrong, rather than reaching out to serve them, you will point at them and ridicule them.

I try to see myself in everyone. When I see someone else struggling with a sin, I don't look down on him or her. I remember when it was me, and that changes how I approach the person. You might not have struggled with the same sins I've struggled with, but you have struggled with something. The Bible says that "all have sinned" (Romans 3:23 NIV). Sometimes we can get so comfortable in our relationship with God and how long we've been in church and how many scriptures we know that we forget how far we once were from Christ.

We must remember to realign. Communion is not only a reminder of the sacrificial suffering and death of Jesus Christ. Communion is also a reminder of our sin, unrighteousness, and separation from God. We need to remember that we were sinners in need of a Savior. If we are going to live on mission, we must never forget the truth about where God brought us from and that He also desires to bring others from darkness into light.

Too Far Gone?

Recall the people God commanded Jonah to call to repentance. These Ninevites were an extremely evil group. In a sense, they were the ISIS of that day, ruthless for no reason. In Jonah's eyes, they did not deserve the grace of God.

If you don't remember how far you once were from Christ, when you see someone who is really out there, you may think that God can't save that person. Even worse, you may put yourself in the place of God and think that this individual does not deserve the very salvation that Jesus died for all to have the opportunity to receive.

Growing up, I loved to watch the video of my father's first sermon. Every time I watched it, I was impressed by how many people were there. He always told me, "Some people weren't there to support me. Some people didn't believe I had become a preacher."

I said, "Dad, what do you mean?"

He began to tell me of his life before Christ. He said that some people thought he was too far gone, that God couldn't reach him and save him and use him to build His kingdom. My mother told me that when she and my father got married, her family made bets on how long they would stay together because of the lifestyle my father led before Jesus Christ. They didn't know that a year later, my father would give his life to Christ.

Then he accepted a call into ministry, and seven months after that, he began pastoring a church. Now he has been serving as senior pastor for over thirty-two years. The same family who thought my father was too far gone now calls on his preacher son to officiate at funerals and weddings!

Don't forget how far you have come and where you once were. Nobody is too far from the hand of God.

The great fish was not Jonah's punishment, but his salvation. It was a manifestation of God's mercy on his life:[6]

> We see it through the entire Bible, life does not come by avoiding death but through death (John 12:24–25); strength comes not despite weakness but in weakness (2 Cor. 12:7–10); comfort comes not by eliminating all affliction but through affliction (2 Cor. 1:3–7).

In a literal sense, if Jonah had stayed at the bottom of the sea, he would have died physically. Had God not rescued Jonah from himself and saved him from the bottom of the sea, the "pit," he would have died spiritually. But God did not leave him in the pit, and would not leave the Ninevites in the pit, either.

Just Tell Your Story

Tell people about how things changed when you gave your life to God. Everything isn't perfect. You are not perfect, and your life isn't everything you want it to be, but things have changed.

You don't have to be a seminary-trained theologian to tell people about Jesus; you just have to tell your story.

If you don't remember when you were at the bottom of the sea, with seaweed wrapped around your head, then you won't tell people about Jesus. If you don't remember when the waves were crashing in on you and you were "sinking deep in sin, far from the peaceful shore,"[7] then you won't tell people about Jesus. If you don't keep that in your heart, you won't answer the call to tell the world that salvation comes only from the Lord. You won't have any motivation to move.

You don't have to be a seminary-trained theologian to tell people about Jesus; you just have to tell your story. If you don't know the story of Adam and Eve, it's all right. If you don't know the story of Abraham, Isaac, and Jacob, it's okay. If you don't know the story of when Jesus walked on water or healed the blind man, that's fine. But it's imperative that you know one story: your story. You need to know the story of how the gospel has changed your life. That is where you start, with your story.

Why? Because you were there. You were there when He healed you, you were there when He delivered you, and you were there when He loved you in spite of yourself. You were right there when He held you close and spoke life into you. You know that story, and that's the only story God calls you to tell.

People don't always want to hear Scripture; they want to hear the story. The story will lead back to the Scriptures. People who don't know Jesus don't understand our Bible. You can give them one hundred scriptures, but if they don't believe the Word, it's not going to mean anything to them. The Bible is not a book you read; it's a book you receive. There are theologians and professors who teach the Bible but don't believe it.

People don't always want to hear Scripture; they want to hear the story.

The gospel does not change those who simply *know* it, but only those who *receive* it. We have to receive its truth about our sin nature that separates us from God and the reality that we cannot, in our own strength, work our way back into relationship with God. We have to believe that salvation comes only by the gift of God through faith and that we are called to live God's way for God's glory.

*The gospel does not change those who simply **know** it, but only those who **receive** it.*

You don't have to explain ten different scriptures to tell your story. Don't be ashamed to say that you were once in the deep. People are impressed with your successes, but they are often more impacted by your failures. People can always identify with someone who messed up: "God delivered you from that? Tell me more about Him."

This is the beauty of it: your story is wrapped in His story. Every time you messed up, every time you lied, every time you did exactly what He told you not to do, it's still a part of His story. If you don't remember where you were, your "chapter one," you won't appreciate and celebrate what God has done for you.

Sometimes when I am on the phone with someone else and my wife is listening to my end of the conversation, she will start whispering to me, "Who are you talking to?" She won't stop until she figures it out.

The world hears our conversation with God, and all they want to know is: Who are you talking to? Tell us about this thing you do every morning called devotions. You are sitting at lunch with that book. What's that about?

Your next step is to get them on the phone with Jesus. They don't have to live through your conversation. They need to get on the phone for themselves. That's all we want to do: connect people to Jesus. Does someone want to know whom you're talking to? Let them say hello for themselves.

Maybe they insist, "No, no, I'm good." That's okay. Keep talking to Jesus and keep telling them your story. You will create a holy curiosity in them that only their own relationship with the Savior can satisfy.

WORKBOOK

Chapter Three Questions

Question: When in your past have you especially struggled with sin? How and through whom did God reach you?

_____

_____

_____

_____

_____

_____

_____

_____

_____

_____

_____

_____

Question: Whom in your life or what groups of people do you tend to consider too far gone for salvation? What are some specific ways you could act more lovingly toward those people?

_____

_____

_____

_____

_____

_____

_____

_____

_____

_____

Question: Who in your life needs to hear your story of salvation? How can you begin to reach that person for God with your story?

_____

_____

_____

_____

_____

_____

_____

_____

_____

_____

_____

Action: There is an urgency to salvation! Don't discount anyone. Remember that you, too, have struggled with sin and falsehood in your past. Don't hesitate or delay in sharing your story with those who are lost!

If you struggle to find the words or to see God's hand in your life, it may help to write out your story and reflect on the main points. However, there's no need to be formal when it comes to telling others; just be yourself.

Chapter Three Notes

CHAPTER FOUR

Obedience to the Call:
God Does Not Want You to Be Awesome, Just Obedient to the Call

How often do you look at the odds of something to determine whether you will or won't take an action? For example, a commercial about medication may boast the ability to fix one health problem, but it also includes ninety-five possible side effects that sound worse than the original issue. You wonder what the odds are of those negative effects occurring.

When I was nineteen, I was in the hospital for some time, and they were talking about doing some surgeries, with a 50/50 chance that the surgeries would either work or make things worse. I said, "No, thank you. I'm okay."

I read once that one in two people have a chance of dealing with cancer. One in four women will miscarry a child. My wife and I lost a baby early on. I had no idea that so many people experience miscarriages.

There is a 1 in 20 chance that you will be a victim of a serious crime. On the other hand, there is a 1 in 36 chance that you could get called down on *The Price Is Right*. The odds of being audited by the IRS are 1 in 175. The odds of becoming a professional athlete are 1 in 22,000 (I've still got a chance!). The odds of becoming a billionaire are only 1 in 7 million.

The odds of getting attacked by a shark are even lower: 1 in 11.5 million, or about five deadly shark attacks per year. Several other animals are statistically much more dangerous. For instance, cows kill people 22 times a year, ants kill people 30 times a year, and deer kill people 130 times a year. Then there are hippos, with 2,900 deadly attacks per year![8]

What are the odds, however, when God enters the picture? Sometimes we don't know what the chances are that when we share our faith, someone will actually listen. Will it work if you tell your story? Will the person really come to Christ? What are the odds?

Unlike with most statistics, when you work with God, the odds are always in your favor. When we obey the Word of God and let Him work through us, awesome things will take place. This truth should motivate Christians to take action all the time. With God on our side, we have a sure chance of seeing miracles happen! Our focus, however, must stay on listening to and following God, not being afraid of what may or may not happen. Say, "God, if this is what You want me to do, then it's what I am going to do, regardless of the human odds."

The odds when working with God are truly awesome. The word *awesome* means to inspire awe. As followers of Christ, we should not focus on being awesome ourselves so that others will be in awe of us. Rather, we should do things according to God's plan so that people will look at Him and stand in awe of who He is.

There is a lost world out there. People are dying spiritually, and God is looking for hearts "fully committed to him" (2 Chronicles 16:9 NIV) and ready to respond to His call.

Availability vs. Ability

> *But I, with shouts of grateful praise, will sacrifice to you. What I have vowed I will make good. I will say, "Salvation comes from the LORD."*
>
> **—Jonah 2:9** *(NIV)*

> *Then the word of the LORD came to Jonah a second time: "Go to the great city of Nineveh and proclaim to it the message I give you."*
>
> *Jonah obeyed the word of the LORD and went to Nineveh. Now Nineveh was a very large city; it took three days to go through it.*
>
> **—Jonah 3:1–3** *(NIV)*

Notice what Jonah was able to say in Jonah 2:9. He vowed to do what God asked him to do. What a change from his previous attitude toward Nineveh!

From the end of chapter 2 to the beginning of chapter 3, Jonah experienced a powerful transformation. He began thinking of others above himself. He committed to obeying God and traveling to one of the worst, most wicked cities in the world at that time, the same city he had refused to go to at the beginning of Jonah chapter 1: *Nineveh.*

Jonah's heart changed because God saved him, and he was able to proclaim, "I, with shouts of grateful praise, will sacrifice to you. What I have vowed I will make good. I will say, 'Salvation comes from the LORD'" (Jonah 2:9 NIV).

In my opinion, this is the most important thing Jonah did in the whole story. He made himself available to God. Scripture says that Jonah finally obeyed God's Word. How are you doing when it comes to availability? Does God have access to your life?

Growing up, I had a friend named Robert, and he and his younger brother, Kwasi, used to come over to my house all the time. My mother would sometimes laugh at Kwasi because when the boys came into the house, Kwasi would go straight to the refrigerator and get whatever he wanted. Not only that, he would be on the house phone and in the refrigerator at the same time.

Kwasi always felt that he had free access to everything—the refrigerator, the pantry, the phone. He didn't feel like he had to ask anybody's permission. He saw everything as available to him, so he didn't have a problem using what he thought he needed at the time. Bottom line: my friend was at home.

Do you give God that kind of access, or do you expect Him to ask permission to use you? God never asked Jonah, "Hey, do you want to go to Nineveh and share your faith?" God instructed Jonah to go, and He expected Jonah to be available and to respond in obedience. If you follow

Christ, He should have access. You should always be available.

Availability is different from ability, however. If you've ever been in a job interview, you might have been asked, "What are your strengths, and what are your weaknesses?" or "What kind of skills and talents do you have?" Do those questions matter regarding your relationship with God?

It's not how many scriptures you know, how long you have been in church, or how much of a people person you are. No, what truly matters to God is your availability, your willingness to say, "God, whatever it is You want me to do, I am available to do that." God will empower you with the ability to do what He has asked you to do.

The apostle Paul wrote of Jesus, "...and he died for all, that those who live might no longer live for themselves but for him who for their sake died and was raised" (2 Corinthians 5:15 ESV). Once you give your life to Christ, your life is no longer about you. If God immediately answered "yes" to every prayer that you have lifted up to Him in the last thirty days, would someone get saved? Would anyone's life be transformed? If not, could it be that you are living for yourself instead of for Christ? Are you not truly making yourself available to Him?

Jesus Christ died so that you would no longer live for yourself, but instead live for Him. You no longer have to walk under the pressure of living by your own skill, education, discipline, or favor.

We Are Part of His Plan

Jesus told Peter, "On this rock I will build my church" (Matthew 16:18 ESV). Jesus is the church builder, not you! The pastor is not called to build the church, either; Christ is. At best, a minister is a custodian. When I start thinking that I am the church builder, I carry the weight of success on my shoulders. But when I say, "Lord, I am available for You to use as You see fit. I am putting Your ability over my ability," there's no room for pride or discouragement.

Every Sunday when we leave church, my wife and I face a huge decision: Where will we eat? That question, if not handled correctly, can destroy the entire day. One minute you can be talking about pancakes, and the next minute, you aren't speaking to each other. Sometimes I will say, "Babe, wherever you want to go," to which she will graciously respond, "No, no, whatever you want to do."

I'm hungry. I want to eat. I really want Mexican food, but we had Mexican on Thursday, and if I tell her that's what I want, she'll remind me that "we just had that." While we are trying to make a decision, I am driving toward the place where I really want to go. Once we are on one side of town, it limits the options. So I am heading in the direction of what I want while claiming, "Babe, whatever you want to do."

Here is the problem: what I'm inadvertently doing is guiding my wife to what I want. Often we try to do the same thing with God. We say, "God, whatever You want me to do," but in our hearts, we're heading in a different direction.

It's your own desires that will hinder your ability and your availability to God. You have to understand that it's not about you, what you want, your plan, or your desire. It's about God's desire.

I'm thankful that God includes us in His plan. The word of the *Lord* came to Jonah. The *Lord* hurled a great wind. The *Lord* appointed a great fish. Salvation belongs to the *Lord*. We get to be a part of *His* plan.

The Past Never Prevents God's Pursuit, Plan, or Purpose

God is not the God of a second chance. He is the God of *another* chance. Some of us wasted our second chance a long, long time ago, but there's always another chance with God.

Notice that the Spirit of the Lord came to Jonah right where he was. Even when we stray, He finds us right where we are and starts over from there. It's like your GPS. If you get off track, the navigation system can still find you. You don't have to go back to your original starting point to get on the right path. The system has the ability to find you right where you are and give you a new path from there. God never fails because He starts from the end and works back to the beginning.

I am so glad that I was not required to be perfect from the day I gave my life to Christ. I am so glad that I was not required to get it right every single time. Any time I wander off the path—any time I decide that I want to get on a boat bound for Tarshish and put other mariners in harm's way—God promises that He will still find me, even at the bottom of the sea.

Your past never stops God from pursuing you. He doesn't wait for you to come crawling back. Notice that God repeated the same directions to Jonah the second time He called him. God still has the same plan for you, even though you may feel like you have forfeited the opportunity to serve Him.

You may be in a place where you can say, "I am not where I should be, but I thank God that I am not where I used to be." God has the same plan and purpose for you; He just has another way to get you there. The path may change, but God's purpose for His children does not.

If we depend on our ability instead of His and things don't go the way we think they should, we think that God doesn't want us anymore because we've failed. This is far from true! God says, in a sense, "I don't care what you did. It doesn't change My pursuit of you. It doesn't change My plan for you. And it definitely doesn't change My purpose for you."

There is nothing in your past so great or so terrible that God will look at it more than He will look at your future. The enemy always reminds us of our past, but God always speaks to our future. So when you are reminded of your past, remember that Jesus Christ died for your sins before you even committed them.

Living a Missional Life

Living a missional life that is others-focused requires a posture before God that is different from what the world promotes. The world says to be strong and to do everything for yourself. However, in God's economy, things work a little differently. Consider what the Bible says about the character of a servant of God.

As we have discussed, a servant of God is **available**. Being available involves humbling yourself before God, giving Him full access to your life, and reconfiguring your life with God and others as the priority.

Paul wrote, "Do nothing from selfishness or empty conceit, but with humility of mind regard one another as more important than yourselves; do not merely look out for your own personal interests, but also for the interests of others" (Philippians 2:3–4 NASB). Before God can work, you must get out of your own way and begin looking to others and their needs.

A servant of God is also **obedient**. It's important to listen intently to the leading of the Holy Spirit, pay attention to what God is telling you to do through His Word, and then actually do it. Jesus said, "You are my friends if you do what I command you" (John 15:14 ESV).

The odds may seem to be against you, and what God is asking may not make sense to you. However, obedience only requires trust in God's will and His plan; you are not responsible for the outcome.

A servant of God **trusts in God's grace and power**. Trust in God's grace as you step out in faith to do what He is asking you to do. Everyone has a messy past, and no one is perfect. People fail, even after putting their faith in Christ. This does not mean that God cannot use you! He will use you in spite of your shortcomings.

> *Obedience only requires trust in God's will and His plan; you are not responsible for the outcome.*

God promises in 2 Corinthians 12:9, "My grace is sufficient for you, for my power is made perfect in weakness" (NIV). Through your weakness, God's power will burst forth. Trust in it! Your ability has nothing to do with the outcome. God is the One who brings the awesomeness to the table, and He will accomplish everything He purposes to do.

Practical Ways to Live a Missional Life

Most people, if they are honest, find it difficult to tell others about Jesus. We don't want to be "that weird Christian." (By the way, if you've never met the weird Christian, you probably *are* the weird Christian!)

Some common reservations I hear include:

- I don't know how to start the conversation.
- I don't want to offend anybody.
- I don't know what to do.

To be *on mission*—that is, actively engaged in sharing your faith, making disciples, baptizing them, and teaching them what Christ has taught you—is not an activity that you set aside time for. It's not a line item on your to-do list. As a follower of Christ, missions should be your lifestyle. You should live your life ready and available to share Christ whenever God prompts you to do so.

A missional life shows your understanding that "the greatest testimony is a life that testifies of God's grace."[9] It's not about telling other people how wrong they are, and if they just do this, everything will change. No. It is a life characterized by sharing God's grace and expressing the love He has shown you.

Be regular. I don't mean normal; I mean regular. Be consistent with your life. For example, go to the same grocery store, coffee shop, gas station, bookstore, etc., and build relationships.

A few years back, when gas prices were going crazy, many of us would almost drive out of gas trying to find the station with the cheapest price. Oftentimes we are so self-serving that we bounce around to different places, looking for sales or discounts but missing opportunities to be missional.

If you consistently go to the same grocery store, there's a good chance that you will see the same people working there. If you keep going there, you may actually learn their names. If you learn their names, sooner or later you may develop some type of relationship. And if you have some type of relationship, you may have some influence.

What I am *not* suggesting is what a friend of mine did. He had just been saved and was looking for ways to share his faith. He prepared to purchase something and told the cashier, "I have a coupon here that's going to save me some money on this. It's kind of like this coupon I got from Jesus Christ." He tried to construct a full-blown gospel presentation out of the coupon one-liner as the cashier stood there, completely weirded out.

I am not suggesting that you use spiritual one-liners to intimidate and harass people.

"Man, it's hot out today!"

"Well, not as hot as it's going to be if you don't get your life straight!"

Rather, ask yourself if there are places you go where you see the same people on a regular basis. Perhaps you've never taken the time to learn their names. Maybe you make eye contact and acknowledge one another with a nod, but you never take it a step further.

Try saying something like, "Hey, what's your name? I've seen you here for the last three years." Just putting in the slight extra effort to learn and use someone's name could change the nature of the relationship and make you stand out from everybody else who comes through the line.

I deliberately take my time talking to the waiter or waitress when my family goes out to eat. I introduce everyone in the family and ask our server, "How are you today?" Every time I do this, I throw off the server's rhythm because no one ever asks that or introduces themselves to waiters and waitresses. No one ever takes the time to say, "Hey, what's going on in your life? You are about to serve me for the next hour, so the least I should do is ask whether you're okay today."

I AM CALLED · 77

What would happen if Christians were to stand out as being people who are consistently more appreciative and considerate than anybody else? Somebody might ask you, "Why do you always care about how I am doing?" You would be able to answer, "This is what Christians are supposed to do." Then you would have an open door to share your faith.

People often notice what they are *seeing* before they hear what you are *saying*. Sometimes we get hung up on using the perfect words and fail to realize that what others observe about us speaks much more loudly than anything we say. If you've seen someone regularly for three years and have never shown any concern for him or her as a person, don't suddenly show up with a scripture to try to win that person to Jesus.

Eat with non-Christians. It's easy to be around people who are like you, who like the same things you like, do the same things you do, and believe the same things you believe. But how are you going to reach people who don't know Christ if you've never spent time with people who don't know Christ?

Everyone eats. Not everyone eats good food or the same quantity or type of food as you eat; however, everyone does eat. Sharing meals helps to create a sense of community and care. Choosing to eat with someone communicates that you want to get to know that person. It's hard to sit with someone and eat for thirty minutes to an hour without talking about anything. I have seen it done, usually by young couples on their phones or older couples who have been married so long that they just have nothing left to talk about.

There may be a neighbor or a co-worker you could invite to eat with you. If you are a student, you could eat with the kids who don't ever have anyone to eat with them or whose friends are at a different lunch. Say, "I hope everything is going well with you today. How are you doing with classes?" Start building a sense of community. Sure, it may be awkward sometimes, but most times it leads to a conversation. When I was a student at North Carolina A&T State University, I led three people to Christ just from sitting down to eat with them.

I learned this approach from Jesus. He was really good at breaking bread with sinners:

> When the teachers of the law who were Pharisees saw him eating with the sinners and tax collectors, they asked his disciples: "Why does he eat with tax collectors and sinners?"
>
> On hearing this, Jesus said to them, "It is not the healthy who need a doctor, but the sick. I have not come to call the righteous, but sinners."
>
> —*Mark 2:16–17* (NIV)

You cannot reach people if you are never in proximity to them. You cannot answer your call in a bubble where you spend time only with people who agree with you. You have to be willing to be around people who don't believe the same things you believe, live the way you live, or talk the way you talk. How are they going to change their lifestyle or their language until they meet Jesus? Maybe they won't meet Jesus if they don't meet you.

Engage your neighbors. This is not about you and whether or not you like your neighbors. If you don't know your neighbors, it's possibly because you don't *want* to know them.

God has placed these people in your life. Figure out a way to serve your neighbors. Maybe they don't cut their grass as often as they should. Maybe you could cut it for them occasionally. Perhaps, like my neighbor, they always park their car in the wrong place, and you can hardly get out of your driveway. The Lord had to work in my heart to help me remember that whether my neighbor knows Jesus is a lot more important than my convenience.

There are many easy ways to create opportunities to get to know your neighbors. Consider the following:

- Organize a get-together.
- Make some popcorn and invite them over for a TV show or a sporting event.
- Organize an ice cream social.
- Have a game night. Everyone likes to relax and have fun!

You could even head up a food or coat drive with the people in your local community. That would both help those in need and encourage new relationships. When you're asked why you're doing it, you have an opportunity to share Jesus. Don't make it a church thing; make it a Jesus thing.

Walk around your neighborhood. You notice things when you walk that you don't notice when you drive. A few months ago, I was walking through the neighborhood, and there were two ladies in a front yard trying to get some branches down without the right tools. I went back to my house, got my pruning shears, and went to help them. All they said at the time was, "You don't have a chainsaw?" A few weeks later, I was out walking, and they ran outside to say, "Thank you for helping us. Why did you stop to help us?" A good deed that seemed unappreciated at the time was sowing seeds for an opportunity to witness later.

How can we share Jesus Christ if we don't know the people who live on our street? You may have people in your neighborhood who already know Christ and could be praying and ministering with you, but because you've never introduced yourself, you don't know who is around you.

Engage your co-workers. Eat with your co-workers. You don't have to do it every day; just pick one day. Perhaps some of your co-workers don't even ask you to go to lunch anymore because you have said "no" so many times. Maybe you need to know them and their stories a little bit better. Maybe you know their stories too well, and that's why you don't want to go to lunch. Go anyway.

Offer to cover for a co-worker's schedule. Help someone who is extra busy with a big project. Remember your co-workers' birthdays. Write encouraging notes for your colleagues, even the ones who have done you wrong. Send a kind email or leave a sticky note on someone's desk. Get to know the janitors and cleaning crew, who are often overlooked. Take a moment to learn their names and ask how they are doing. These are simple things you can do to create an open door without being that weird Christian.

Get involved in your local community. Participate in community-wide celebrations. Invite your church family to your community events. Take advantage of volunteer opportunities and you will begin to connect and engage with people you never would have met any other way. Find a local non-profit organization you appreciate and partner with it.

Impact Steps

Stepping out in faith and trusting God to work isn't always easy, but remember that the odds are in your favor when you are walking with God. The Holy Spirit dwelling within you will empower you to do what you don't think you can do on your own.

There are a few simple steps to remember as you seek to live a missional life for Christ.

Intercede. Before you try to reach out to somebody, take a moment to pray. Spend some time praying for your neighbors, family members, and co-workers.

Invest. The greatest investment you can make in someone is sharing your grace story of how God loved you and chose to use you in spite of your sins and flaws. None of our stories are perfect, but share the story you have. Maybe somebody will ask you an incredible question about why you do what you do. That's a wonderful opportunity to invest in that person.

Invite. Invite people into prayer. They don't have to pray with you; just offer to pray for them. Few people are offended by prayer. You can also invite them to a church service or an event, but keep the focus on inviting them to

Jesus. Church has healed no one, but Jesus, through His blood, can heal everyone!

All these different things are not self-benefiting. If you're going to answer the call that Christ has on your life, you truly have to deny yourself and follow God and His plan for your days. We have so many excuses and so many reasons why we don't share our faith or why people don't know Jesus. Maybe we think that the first thing they have to do is come to church, and that's not true.

Make the decision to live a missional life. Choose three things that you can do, starting now. If we don't take the time to look at these practical, very small, very simple things, we will never do anything. We will always say, "If only…" or "I should have" or "I could have." If we get outside of ourselves, the odds with God are absolutely awesome that He will use us to impact the community around us for Him.

Being Obedient Over Being Awesome

Jonah began by going a day's journey into the city, proclaiming, "Forty more days and Nineveh will be overthrown." The Ninevites believed God. A fast was proclaimed, and all of them, from the greatest to the least, put on sackcloth.

When Jonah's warning reached the king of Nineveh, he rose from his throne, took off his royal robes, covered himself with sackcloth and sat down in the dust.

—Jonah 3:4–6 (NIV)

Perhaps you have been hesitant to step out in faith and rely on God's power to change lives because the voices in your head are saying:

- "I'm just not good enough."
- "I told God I would never, ever sin in that way again, but I did it twice the first chance I got."
- "If I were like [this other person], then God would definitely use me."
- "I am just not awesome enough."

These voices can drown out God's voice, and they certainly do not speak life or truth to your soul.

God never asked you to be awesome. God just wants you to be obedient.

When I was young, my teacher would ask me what I wanted to be when I grew up, and I would answer, "Awesome." It was either that or a PE teacher (because they got to wear basketball shorts to work).

Some teachers thought that I was just being smart, but I was being honest. We all want to be awesome. But even when it seems that everything is going right for you, you will always feel like you can do more. You can probably recall a time when you did something really well, but within a few days, you were discouraged because you were terrible at something else.

Let me free you today. God never asked you to be awesome. God just wants you to be obedient.

Let's circle back to Jonah's journey. Jonah's call to repentance reached the Ninevites, and "the Ninevites believed God" (Jonah 3:5 NIV). When the king of the Ninevites heard Jonah's warning, he "covered himself with sackcloth and sat down in the dust" (Jonah 3:6 NIV). In ancient biblical times, when people covered themselves in sackcloth (often rolling in ashes as well), it meant that they were mourning over evil or humbly repenting of sin.

The government of Nineveh was transformed as a result of Jonah's simple, eight-word sermon (five words in Hebrew[10]): "Forty more days and Nineveh will be overthrown" (Jonah 3:4 NIV). Revival broke out.

Jonah didn't need to be awesome. He didn't even have to be really good. What did he have to be? He had to be obedient. It wasn't Jonah who did this work in the people; it was God. God is not asking you to be awesome. He is not asking you to be a superhero. God is not asking you to be super-spiritual or super-deep. He is asking, "Will you be obedient?" If you choose to be obedient, God can do something awesome.

Some of us think that we have to do something awesome for God to love us. We are trying to impress Him. It's not what you do that makes you awesome in the sight of God; it's just the fact that you are who you are. He loves you just as you are, and that is truly awesome.

Most of us, if we'd been sent to Nineveh, would have been standing in the public square, spouting warnings and scriptures, slapping the Bible—and distracting from God's message. We don't need a dozen scriptures, a whole book of Proverbs, or a lot of "Christianese" expressions. We only need to proclaim the message God gave us.

Jonah finally seemed to figure this out. He walked in obedience, and God changed an entire city. If only the book of Jonah ended there!

Chapter Four Questions

Question: When have you tried to depend on your own strength rather than on God? How did it turn out? How could you have prioritized obedience over awesomeness?

_____

_____

_____

_____

_____

_____

_____

_____

_____

_____

_____

Question: What are some specific ways you can make yourself more available to your neighbors and community for God?

_____

_____

_____

_____

_____

_____

_____

_____

_____

Question: When have you seen God's transforming awesomeness at work in your life and the lives of others?

_____

_____

_____

_____

_____

_____

_____

_____

_____

_____

_____

Action: Remember that you are a part of God's plan. It's less important to feel able and awesome in your own capacity and more important to be available for Him to work through in His perfect ability. Don't try to depend on yourself, but rather trust and obey Him. Make yourself available for His purposes and the mission He has for you.

Consider how you can engage with others, pray for them, invest in them, and invite them to join you in practicing spiritual disciplines, such as prayer and Bible study. Draw up an action plan of how, through God's grace, you can have an impact for Him in the lives of those around you.

Chapter Four Notes

_____

_____

_____

_____

_____

_____

_____

_____

_____

_____

_____

_____

_____

_____

_____

_____

_____

_____

_____

_____

_____

_____

CHAPTER FIVE

A Heart for the Call:
Challenged and Changed by the Call

When Jonah's warning reached the king of Nineveh, he rose from his throne, took off his royal robes, covered himself with sackcloth and sat down in the dust. This is the proclamation he issued in Nineveh: "By the decree of the king and his nobles: Do not let people or animals, herds or flocks, taste anything; do not let them eat or drink. But let people and animals be covered with sackcloth. Let everyone call urgently on God. Let them give up their evil ways and their violence. Who knows? God may yet relent and with compassion turn from his fierce anger so that we will not perish." When God saw what they did and how they turned from their evil ways, he relented and did not bring on them the destruction he had threatened.
—Jonah 3:6–10 (NIV)

Recall that wearing sackcloth and ashes was an outward sign of a repentant heart. The king said that not only the people, but even the animals needed to wear sackcloth. I guess it's one thing when you ask God for forgiveness and repent, but when you make your dog repent, you are serious!

Wouldn't this be a great place to end the book of Jonah? This is where the theme song is supposed to come back in, the credits are supposed to roll, and everyone is happy. The Ninevites gave their hearts to God, and God decided not to destroy them.

But there is no ignoring Jonah chapter 4.

More Than Sharing Your Faith

But to Jonah this seemed very wrong, and he became angry. He prayed to the LORD, "Isn't this what I said, LORD, when I was still at home? That is what I tried to forestall by fleeing to Tarshish."

—Jonah 4:1–2 (NIV)

The Ninevites did what they were supposed to do. They repented. This is one of the most successful revivals in the history of the world. So why do we have another chapter to this book? Shouldn't the story end there?

It doesn't end there because Jonah still had a heart issue. Jonah did not want these people to have a relationship with God. He wanted God to bring His wrath on them!

You can do good work with the wrong heart. You can do God's will, yet still try to control it. Have there ever been people you didn't truly want God to save? Maybe you have thought, "Lord, okay, I hope they get saved, but don't let me see them in heaven because I won't forget what they did to me." Sometimes we don't honestly want certain people to know Jesus because then we would have to forgive them and love them and have fellowship with them.

I AM CALLED · 93

I have a younger sister named Megan who, like most younger siblings, could always get away with things I couldn't. I told her the other day, "You have liquid gold in your eyes." If my father sees Megan cry, suddenly everything is possible for her. Growing up, I would be so hopeful that she was "gonna get it." I did something, and my father lost his mind over it. But when my sister did the same thing, he would say, "Come here, baby. It's all right."

Some of us don't want to have a heart like God's because God's heart is full of grace.

Sometimes we live the Christian life that way. We see someone who's not living right get a blessing that we have spent years praying for and still don't have. We serve and lead and are faithful, yet we seem to go through one trial after the next, while this other person who isn't obeying the Word seems to have a perfect, tranquil life. In the same way, Jonah was upset because these evil people found favor with God.

You have to have the heart of God if you are going to answer the call of God. Some of us don't want to have a heart like God's because God's heart is full of grace. Jonah didn't want to go tell Nineveh about God's goodness. He did not want to give them God's warning because he knew that God would extend grace. Though obedient, Jonah's heart did not reflect God's character.

Remember that Jonah was a prophet, one of the mouthpieces for God in his day. Even so, he complained to God, "I knew that you are a gracious and compassionate God, slow to anger and abounding in love, a God who relents from sending calamity. Now, LORD, take away my life, for it is better for me to die than to live" (Jonah 4:2–3 NIV). In effect, he was saying, "Lord, if they are going to live, I would rather die."

Answering the call is not just about sharing our faith. What do you do once people give their lives to Christ? Where is your heart when they heed God's warning? How do you feel when your enemy gives his or her life to Christ? Do you extend compassion and grace?

Moved by God's Care

Everything in these first four verses of Jonah 4 is about how Jonah felt:

- "I am angry."
- "I feel like this is wrong."
- "I knew this would happen!"

Every Christian needs to pray, "Lord, help me to care for the things You care for." It's an interesting turn in the text because just two chapters before, Jonah himself needed grace and compassion—the same grace and compassion that the people of Nineveh needed—when he was in the belly of a fish. If that's the case, why was Jonah so angry?

The Ninevites, otherwise known as the Assyrians, were Israel's worst enemy. Jonah believed that God should be bringing judgment on the enemies of His chosen people, not extending grace to them! Jonah knew that God's character is full of grace and compassion. This was why he wanted to flee to Tarshish in the first place. He knew that God would extend forgiveness to the Ninevites if they were to repent, and Jonah wanted none of it.

Have you ever felt that grace is just for you and other people who live the way you do, for people of your culture or race? When you become envious of favor that God shows to somebody else, it destroys your heart.

Another potential reason for Jonah's anger was that he had just proclaimed that God's wrath was coming, so when it didn't come, that made him look like a false prophet. If it were happening today, we would say that he was going to be disinvited to all the revivals and special conferences he had just booked. He might have been more concerned with his image than God's.

A third possible reason for Jonah's wrath was that he might not have believed that the Ninevites could truly turn and live righteously. He thought that they would continue to attack others and do their damage across the region. Sometimes we have the same feelings about people of other religions or those who profess no belief in God.

Maybe they are doing things that are evil in the sight of God, but that doesn't mean we aren't still supposed to love them. We can disagree with people and call their sin what it is without distancing ourselves or praying for God to judge them. But sometimes we want the wrath of God to come on them instead of saying, "Lord, we want Your grace to cover them so they might see You."

God is not always going to call you to lead people to Christ whom you want to see led to Christ. Maybe it's that co-worker who sits beside you, the one you've been praying would get transferred across the country or let go from the job. Maybe God has that co-worker sitting right beside you every day, sharing his story and telling you stuff that you don't even want to know about, because He needs you to share Christ with him. Maybe the people who did you wrong had to do you wrong so you could forgive them and love them in spite of themselves, and they would see the love of Christ in how you treat them.

Moved by God's Compassion

> *But the LORD replied, "Is it right for you to be angry?"*
>
> *Jonah had gone out and sat down at a place east of the city. There he made himself a shelter, sat in its shade and waited to see what would happen to the city.*
> —*Jonah 4:4–5 (NIV)*

God's compassion for others should be our motivator for loving people who are hard to love. Jesus Christ showed His compassion for us when He died on the cross on our behalf. It wasn't just something He said or felt; it's something He showed us. The perfect, blameless life He lived for thirty-three years and His undeserved death on the cross allowed Him to be the Lamb slain for our sins.

Jesus said, "A new commandment I give to you, that you love one another: just as I have loved you, you also are to love one another" (John 13:34 ESV). Jesus commands His followers to love. We are called to share what we have been shown. He is not just our motivation, but also our model.

Compassion is care with action. Compassion is the legs, the hands, and the arms of care. While care is how you *feel*, compassion is what you *do*.

God's compassion for others should be our motivator for loving people who are hard to love.

Jonah was so angry that Scripture says he constructed a shelter outside of Nineveh and basically sulked. After Jonah had his temper tantrum, God stepped in and asked him, "Is it right for you to be angry?" (Jonah 4:4 NIV).

Jonah wanted to see what was really going to happen. He was probably thinking, "Lord, I know You are actually going to destroy them, right? I know Your wrath is going to come. Lord, that's what You told me, and I want to be here to see it. I don't want to be *in* there, but man, I can't wait to watch this unfold!"

Have you ever felt like just sitting back and watching people get what was coming to them? Did you want to see that boss who wrongly fired you receive just punishment? Have you ever been the one sitting in the shade, waiting for the Lord to crash someone's world to the ground? That person who abused you, that person who deceived you, the one who broke your heart—you want a front-row seat to God "getting them" for how they did you wrong.

However, God's heart is not man's heart. His heart is full of care and compassion. Notice how God responded to Jonah's ugly heart:

> Then the LORD God provided a leafy plant and made it grow up over Jonah to give shade for his head to ease his discomfort, and Jonah was very happy about the plant.
> —*Jonah 4:6 (NIV)*

God sent Jonah a plant to make him more comfortable—and to teach him a lesson. What was Jonah's discomfort? He was out there without a house, and it was cold at night and hot during the day. This plant saved him from his discomfort. It covered him as God's grace covers us. But God was not done teaching Jonah:

> But at dawn the next day God provided a worm, which chewed the plant so that it withered. When the sun rose, God provided a scorching east wind, and the sun blazed on Jonah's head so that he grew faint. He wanted to die, and said, "It would be better for me to die than to live."
>
> But God said to Jonah, "Is it right for you to be angry about the plant?"
>
> "It is," he said. "And I'm so angry I wish I were dead."
>
> But the LORD said, "You have been concerned about this plant, though you did not tend it or make it grow. It sprang up overnight and died overnight. And should I not have concern for the great city of Nineveh, in which there are more than a hundred and twenty thousand people who

cannot tell their right hand from their left—and also many
animals?"

—Jonah 4:7–11 (NIV)

Jonah cared more about the plant than about the people. Why? Because it covered him. Many of us are angry when the shade and comfort of our lives are gone, yet we aren't upset at the idea that someone could be lost. Jonah was ready to die because the thing that protected him and made him comfortable was taken away, but when God extended grace to undeserving sinners, he was angry.

God was saying of the 120,000 in Nineveh, "How can I not extend them grace? They've never been taught any better." Some of us don't even have grace for people who haven't done anything wrong or who don't know that they are doing wrong. Whether the 120,000 people were physical babies or also adults who were spiritual infants, these Ninevites didn't know right from wrong. They didn't know God's Word, and they didn't know God's will. We, like Jonah, may want to see His righteous justice, but God says no. Grace is enough. The grace that God has shared in your life, the grace you had nothing to do with and did nothing to deserve, is the same grace that He wants to share in others' lives.

God's Heart for Reconciliation

Why does God not respond in revenge as we are inclined to do? Because God's heart is a heart of reconciliation. The ultimate act of reconciliation is seen in the death of God's Son, Jesus, who reconciled a lost world back to Him. Paul wrote:

> *All this is from God, who reconciled us to himself through Christ and gave us the ministry of reconciliation: that God was reconciling the world to himself in Christ, not counting people's sins against them. And he has committed to us the message of reconciliation.*
> **—2 Corinthians 5:18–19** *(NIV)*

Since God reconciled us back to Him, though we were still sinners, we should also press into the ministry of reconciliation toward others. Why? Because reconciliation reflects the heart of God.

The word *reconciliation* indicates restoration. God saw you in the belly of a fish, in the darkest parts of the sea, separated from Him because of your own sin, and He brought you back. Now you have the responsibility of extending compassion to help others experience this same reconciliation with God.

I thank God that He doesn't count my sins against me! In the same way, I shouldn't count other people's sins against them. We are called to tell others, "God wants you back! With all of your sin, with all of your mess, Jesus Christ died on the cross so you and God could have a relationship."

Paul also wrote, "We are therefore Christ's ambassadors, as though God were making his appeal through us. We implore you on Christ's behalf: Be reconciled to God" (2 Corinthians 5:20 NIV). If you have a relationship with Jesus Christ, He is trying to make His appeal through you.

This is why missions and evangelism are not an event, a day's work, or even a ministry—they're your life!

Reconciliation between God and humankind through Christ restores what was lost through sin. Sin separates, but reconciliation brings back together. God the Father cares about vertical reconciliation, meaning our reconciliation with Him. Without this, there can never be horizontal reconciliation among brothers and sisters in Christ of all nations, tribes, and tongues. Through His death, Christ tore down the dividing walls of hostility (Galatians 3:28).

Missions and evangelism are not an event, a day's work, or even a ministry—they're your life!

The horizontal cross post always hangs on the vertical cross post. When the Pharisees asked Jesus what the most important commandment was, Jesus answered that the first was to love God and the second was to "love your neighbor as yourself" (Matthew 22:35–40 NIV). It's vertical first, horizontal second. Our first responsibility is to come to God, and then we are able to come together with others.

One of the first Bibles I received as a teenager was the God's Word Translation. I love how this version translates 2 Corinthians 5:18–20 (GW):

> *God has done all this. He has restored our relationship with him through Christ, and has given us this ministry of restoring relationships. In other words, God was using Christ to restore his relationship with humanity. He didn't hold people's faults against them, and he has given us this message of restored relationships to tell others. Therefore, we are Christ's representatives, and through us God is calling you. We beg you on behalf of Christ to become reunited with God.*

Every enemy, every foe, every person who did you wrong, every family member you don't like—your responsibility is to help them restore their relationship with God through Jesus Christ. That's our ministry!

When I started Vertical Church, people were constantly asking me, "Are we going to have this kind of ministry? Are we going to host this group? Are we going to do this? Are we going to do that?"

I answered, "You are making it about you. I am here to make sure you meet Jesus, and if you meet Jesus, He will meet your needs."

Relationship Restorer

If you are a follower of Christ, your job description is "relationship restoration." Are you worried that you don't know what your purpose is, what you're supposed to do in your life? There it is. Write it down, highlight it in your Bible, Snapchat it, Instagram, whatever you do to note something: "Start a relationship." There are different tools and different ways to do that, but at the end of the day, your purpose is about restoring relationships. Scripture does not say that man uses Christ to restore a relationship with God; it says that God uses Christ to restore a relationship with man.

When you are dating somebody and it's starting to get serious, there comes a pivotal point in the relationship where somebody has to be the first one to say, "I love you." Conventional wisdom says not to be the one who says it first because it makes you look like you are in need. Regardless, I'm so glad that God didn't wait for me to say, "I love you," before He sent His Son to die on a cross for my sins! He wanted a restored relationship with us more than we wanted it with Him.

When you hold people's faults against them, you won't serve them, bless them, or love them. God doesn't hold it against them, so why should you? Your unforgiveness is a wall between you and a person who needs the love of Jesus Christ. You can wear the chains of unforgiveness for so long that they start to feel like jewelry. Soon you can't tell your enemies that God loves them because you don't want to believe that He does.

God has not given us the message that "you are wrong" or "God is displeased with you" or "God is sick of you." It's the message that even though you are wrong, God still loves you. Many people miss Jesus Christ because the only message that the church wants to give is how wrong they are.

We are Christ's representatives. To be a representative means to "re-present" someone or something to others. Every day you should re-present Jesus Christ—re-present His values, re-present His mercy, re-present His love, re-present His grace, and re-present the message of Jesus Christ.

What would you act like if you always had to wear a shirt that read, "I am a representative of Christ"? Everywhere you went, you would be visibly marked as speaking and acting on Christ's behalf. Would your attitude change? People don't know what Jesus Christ looks like; they just know what *you* look like. Christ is trying to get His message to people through us.

My dad is a pastor, and there were times when he would do three or four services on a Sunday. I would decide that I'd had enough and go to the house of anyone who would take me. My mom and dad would say, "Don't go over there and embarrass us." When I was heading to school, they would say, "Don't make us have to come up there because you've embarrassed us." I had a responsibility to re-present my parents and my family wherever I went.

This is why we need the process of sanctification to mold us, develop us, and mature us into better representatives. Lord, forgive me for the times when I've embarrassed You. Forgive me if I've gone into the world and been a poor representation of who You are.

A Heart Like His

Anyone can do a good work with the wrong heart. Answer your call, but always look at your heart.

I am not sharing my faith to tell people that God is going to destroy them and they are going to hell. I don't want to scare people into heaven. I have a message that if you give your life to Christ, you don't have to wait until eternity; you can experience the glory of God in your life right now. You can experience a relationship with God right now. This is my prayer for you: that you would understand that God has given you the message of restoration, not the message of division.

Once you become a child of God, you have His heart. Scripture promises that when you put your faith in Christ, God "give[s] you a new heart and put[s] a new spirit in you" (Ezekiel 36:26 NIV). Paul wrote, "I have been crucified with Christ; and it is no longer I who live, but Christ lives in me; and the life which I now live in the flesh I live by faith in the Son of God, who loved me and gave Himself up for me" (Galatians 2:20 NASB).

The greatest testimony is a life lived with grace.

Once you have vertical reconciliation with God through Jesus Christ, then horizontal reconciliation—racial reconciliation, ethnic reconciliation, socioeconomic reconciliation, and gender reconciliation—become possible through Him.

God saw us in our mess, extended grace, cared for us, and had compassion. May He break our hearts with the things that break His heart. "While we were still sinners, Christ died for us" (Romans 5:8 NIV)—not for some of us, not for the good people, not for the right people, not for some special people, but for all of us.

Lord, help us to express the truth of the gospel with our lives. The greatest testimony is a life lived with grace.

May God employ us in the ministry of relationship restoration.

WORKBOOK

Chapter Five Questions

Question: Who in your life or community is especially hurting right now? How can you show godly compassion to that person?

_____

_____

_____

_____

_____

_____

_____

_____

_____

_____

Question: How well do you represent Christ? How could you better represent Him and His heart in your daily life?

_____

_____

_____

_____

_____

_____

_____

_____

_____

Question: If you had to write a specific job description for yourself as a "relationship restorer," what would it include?

_____

_____

_____

_____

_____

_____

_____

_____

_____

_____

_____

Action: Don't be content to do good works with a wrong heart. To answer the call of God, examine yourself continually to ensure that you maintain the heart of God. Be moved by God's care and compassion, avoiding the temptation to despise or resent other people. Ask God to show you where your thoughts and attitudes toward others fail to reflect His grace so that you can truly "re-present" His love for them. Have a heart of reconciliation and forgiveness as you work every day to restore relationships, especially the relationship between God and His children.

Chapter Five Notes

CONCLUSION

Fully Committed

There are many good things in which Christians may be involved. Ministry opportunities abound, and human needs are endless. Every day, we must make multiple decisions about how we will spend our time, whom we will talk to, and whom we will share Christ with. Personal wants, needs, and desires play into almost every decision we make. Often we find ourselves overworked, overbooked, and overcommitted as we try desperately to do the will of God in our own strength while dying on the vine at the same time.

God's call is not and should not be difficult. It comes in the form of a quiet voice (1 Kings 19:12) that aligns with God's Word and His character, instructing believers in the way we should go. Consider these words from the prophet Isaiah:

Whether you turn to the right or to the left, your ears will hear a voice behind you, saying, "This is the way; walk in it."

—*Isaiah 30:21 (NIV)*

God's call is for the believer to walk closely with Him, to be in intimate relationship with Him, and to do what He asks—nothing more. It won't always be comfortable, and sometimes it may be the exact opposite of what the believer would choose to do. But His ways are good, and His purposes will stand. Whether a person chooses to obey God or not, His plans *will* come to pass.

Every day, we are faced with a choice: to follow God or to follow our own desires. As with Jonah, how we choose to respond will affect not only ourselves, but also others. Those who choose to respond in obedience to God will experience the joy of seeing God work in unimaginable ways. And it will be simple; it won't feel like work. But this takes a commitment to set aside self, to be available for Him to use, and to trust Him for what cannot be seen.

Though Jonah exhibited bouts of obedience, his heart was not fully committed to God's purposes and plans. By contrast, I challenge you today to respond in obedience to God's call on your life with a heart fully committed to Him. Ask God for a heart like His, a heart full of grace, care, compassion, and reconciliation. The impact on others will be more than you could ever imagine!

REFERENCES

Notes

1. Wesley, John. *Minutes of Several Conversations, Between the Rev. John Wesley, A.M., and the Preachers in Connexion with Him: Containing the Form of Discipline Established Among the Preachers and People in the Methodist Societies.* Reprint of 1797 edition. Methodist Book-Room, 1797, p. 13.

2. Cecil, Richard, and John Newton. *The Works of the Rev. John Newton: Containing a Authentic Narrative ... to Which Are Prefixed, Memoirs of His Life &c.* Vol. 1. R. Carter, 1847, p. 62.

3. Brown, John. "Jonah 2." In Blue Letter Bible. https://www.blueletterbible.org/Comm/brown_john/Jon/Jonah_3.cfm.

4. Kellogg, Grace W. *The Bible Today.* In J. Vernon McGee, *Through the Bible.* Vol. 3. Thomas Nelson, 1984, p. 752–753. https://www.blueletterbible.org/Comm/brown_john/Jon/Jonah_3.cfm.

5. *Expository Dictionary of Bible Words*, "1644. garash." Edited by Stephen D. Renn. Hendrickson Publishers, 2005.

6. *ESV Gospel Transformation Bible* (Commentary). Crossway, 2013, p. 1196.

7. Rowe, James. "Love Lifted Me." 1912. In *Evening Light Songs*. Faith Publishing House, 1949. http://library.timelesstrut hs.org/music/Love_Lifted_Me.

8. Barnett, Heather. "What Are the Odds? 21 Statistics That Will Surprise You." SheKnows.com. 2013. http://www.sheknows.com/living/articles/1023453/what-are-the-odds-21-statistics-that-will-surprise-you.

9. Gray, Derwin L. *The High Definition Leader: Building Multiethnic Churches in a Multiethnic World*. Thomas Nelson, 2015.

10. "Jonah 3:4." Bible Hub. http://biblehub.com/text/jonah/3-4.htm.

About the Author

Ryan Brooks serves as the Lead Pastor and founder of Vertical Church in Hillsborough, NC. Vertical Church is a Christ-centered, multi-ethnic, multigenerational church seeking to make disciples who make disciples. Ryan serves on several boards of local organizations, along with being a ministry coach to several pastors and churches across the country. Ryan is married to his best friend, April Brooks, and they have four children—Darian, Brandon, Wesley, and London Grace.

About Sermon To Book

SermonToBook.com began with a simple belief: that sermons should be touching lives, *not* collecting dust. That's why we turn sermons into high-quality books that are accessible to people all over the globe.

Turning your sermon series into a book exposes more people to God's Word, better equips you for counseling, accelerates future sermon prep, adds credibility to your ministry, and even helps make ends meet during tight times.

John 21:25 tells us that the world itself couldn't contain the books that would be written about the work of Jesus Christ. Our mission is to try anyway. Because in heaven, there will no longer be a need for sermons or books. Our time is now.

If God so leads you, we'd love to work with you on your sermon or sermon series.

Visit www.sermontobook.com to learn more.